BIBLICAL REFLECTIONS
ON CRISES FACING THE CHURCH

I dedicate this book
with gratitude
to

The President and Board of Trustees of
DE PAUL UNIVERSITY, Chicago
for the Honorary Doctorate of Humane Letters
granted to me in November 1974

and to

The President and Board of Trustees of
VILLANOVA UNIVERSITY, Philadelphia
for the Honorary Doctorate of Letters
granted to me in May 1975

Biblical Reflections
on
Crises Facing the Church

by
Raymond E. Brown, S.S.

PAULIST PRESS
New York, N.Y./Paramus, N.J.

NIHIL OBSTAT
Myles M. Bourke, S.T.D., S.S.L.
Censor Deputatus

IMPRIMATUR
✠James P. Mahoney, D.D.
Vicar General, Archdiocese of New York

June 27, 1975

Library of Congress
Catalog Card Number: 75-19861

ISBN 0-8091-1891-2

Published by Paulist Press
Editorial Office: 1865 Broadway, N.Y., N.Y. 10023
Business Office: 400 Sette Drive, Paramus, N.J. 07652

Printed and bound in the
United States of America

Contents

Preface

In our times biblical reflections should stem from a study of the Bible that is as scientifically accurate as possible. And so I make no apologies that this is a book that assumes the acceptability of modern biblical criticism. Biblical criticism is no panacea; even as a scientific discipline it has limitations that the twenty-first century will be very happy to point out. But imperfect tool that it may be, it remains the surest means of learning how God has acted in the history of Israel, in Jesus of Nazareth, and in the first-century Church.

Working alone, one can master biblical criticism and reflect on the implications of the Bible for our times; but as a Roman Catholic my religious sensibilities dictate that biblical reflection is best done in the context of a believing community, the Church. This is not always an easy vocation. The Roman Catholic Church spent the first third of this century in opposition to biblical criticism; it spent the second third of the century accepting biblical criticism; only now, in the last third of the century, is it really facing the problem of how to live with the impact of biblical criticism. It may sound grandiose to say that the Church has to come to terms with the impact of biblical criticism, but I think it crucial that what the Church thinks about the Bible should affect its religious outlook. And biblical criticism, when it really works, results in a very different way of thinking about the Bible than has been customary in the Church.

I do not mean that the voice of Scripture, critically studied, is the only voice that the Church has to live with and respond to. The voice of Tradition (i.e., church experience and thought in the centuries after the first) has also to have its say. But I do not think that the voice of subsequent Tradition should drown out the voice of Scripture, the tradition of the first century. Nor do I think that we should be allowed to gloss over the tensions between the two on the dubious principle that the Spirit always says the same thing. Only when each has had its say, resonant with all the sharpness of the tension between them, can the Church of our times face its crises with the fullness of Christian experience brought to bear. Scripture is not the master of the Church; but when it is allowed to speak freely, it can serve as the nagging conscience of the Church.

In my intellectual career I was fortunate enough to miss that first third of the century when the Roman Catholic Church stood in opposition to biblical criticism. By the time I came on the scene of biblical study, my Church was already accepting the methodology of biblical criticism. Perhaps that is why it has come naturally to me to have a positive attitude toward the Church's authority, which I have found friendly and not repressive in my biblical growth. That growth was slow enough in those middle years of the century from *Divino Afflante Spiritu* (1943) till Vatican II (1962-65) that I have retained a sympathy for people who need to be moved gradually in matters biblical. In these lectures I try to make their journey easier by showing that there is a foundation in church teaching for the biblical route that we are taking. If there is an impatience in this book, it is not with Catholics who need time to make a personal adjustment to the Church's change of attitude toward biblical criticism; my impatience is with those who want to move us back to the first third of the century by repressing the freedom that the Church has gradually granted to biblical criticism.

But if I had the good fortune to grow up with the Church in the second third of this century, I recognize that a moment of great intellectual adventure in learning method and facts is not one that can be prolonged forever, either for an individual or for the Church. For one whose vocation is the hyphenated vocation of priest-teacher, the leisure of a descriptive study of the Scriptures must ultimately be impinged upon by the pressure of significance. Now that Catholics have joined the majority of their Christian brothers and sisters in a relatively common understanding of the New Testament, they must inevitably face the question of what our more accurate knowledge of Jesus and the early Church means for the Church and the Christian today— the question of the last third of the century. The chapters of this book are my attempts to grapple with that question on prominent occasions in the last two years: when I was asked to give a keynote address on the problems of religious education to the National Catholic Educational Association; when I spoke on christology to the national convention of the College Theology Society, and especially when I was invited to give the Hoover Lectures at the University of Chicago on the future of ecumenism.

The last-mentioned occasion particularly pleased me since in recent years I have had the grace of teaching Protestant students for the ministry as well as Catholic candidates for the priesthood. The Roman Catholic Church could not have made its advance in biblical criticism without Protestant aid. In the first third of the century the torch of biblical criticism was kept lighted by Protestant scholars; and when after 1943 Catholics lit their candles from it, they profited from the burnt fingers as well as the glowing insights of their Protestant confreres. It is no accident that Protestant and Catholic biblical scholars have been coming closer together ever since, to the point now of producing common studies of divisive problems. Such ecumenical experience governs the themes in this book, for I hope and pray that the ultimate goal of the Roman Catholic biblical pilgrimage in the twentieth century will be a unified Christianity. The Scriptures critically studied will not have had the impact they should have on the churches if the second millenium closes on a Christianity as divided as it is now.

The word "crises" appears in my title. To some a crisis is an unsettling disaster, and the crises they find described on the front pages of their secular and religious newspapers are a sign that both country and church are falling apart. But in the biblical sense a *krisis* is a moment of judgment, and there never was a crisis so great as when Jesus of Nazareth proclaimed the inauguration of God's rule among men. The Master whose initial coming was a *krisis* may be speaking again to his people in the crises of today, and an informed reflection on the Bible may enable us to discern his voice. It is my hope that this small collection of lectures may aid in that cause.

PART ONE

CRISES IN THEOLOGY

1.
The Current Crisis in Theology as it Affects the Teaching of Catholic Doctrine[1]

In this address I wish, first, to explain why there is a type of crisis in theology today, and, second, to discuss how this affects the teaching of Catholic doctrine. Of course, I do not pretend to have a *complete* insight into either the theological crisis or its effect on doctrinal teaching, nor do I pretend that I can give totally satisfactory solutions. I shall be quite satisfied if I can add to our mutual understanding of theological development and doctrinal teaching, for I think that one of the greatest dangers facing the Roman Catholic Church today is a polarization arising from a lack of understanding.

THE CRISIS IN THEOLOGY

Let me begin with the crisis implicit in current Catholic theological development. Theology is an attempt to give expression to our faith in God and our understanding of how He has worked in the world. In the course of Christian history theology

---

[1]The keynote address at the April 1973 convention of the National Catholic Educational Association at New Orleans (and reported in the April 19th issue of *Origins*, the National Catholic Documentary Service). The address is reproduced without change here but with the addition of some footnotes.

has developed, not smoothly but in spurts. Too often, in describing theological development, we have used the imagery of a mainstream flowing smoothly down the ages, fed by gentle rains and small tributaries. But if one wishes to use the river imagery, a much truer historical picture would be that of a stream, at times placid and even sluggish, but at other times violently agitated by floodwaters, as swollen tributaries pour into it their soil-laden currents, changing its color and even the direction of its flow. By the tributaries I mean the great contributions to Christian theology at various periods of history when new bodies of knowledge were made part of our religious heritage. One may think of the upheaval in Christian theology in the fourth to the sixth centuries as the tributary of Greco-Roman knowledge, especially Platonic philosophy, gave new color and direction to teachings that had their headwaters in a Semitic world. Or again, the upheaval that occurred in the high Middle Ages when Aristotelian thought, which came by the route of Arabian commentators and Christian thinkers, like Thomas Aquinas, poured into the Christian mainstream and once more changed the hue and direction. Or even the sixteenth century when both the Reformation and the Renaissance had their turbulent effect on Catholic theology.

And in every period of major theological change there has been resistance to the new ideas and the new knowledge that were being put to the service of Christianity. We must not forget how bitterly opposed in their own times were the inaugurators of Catholic theological progress, even if later centuries justified them. Jerome's magnificent attempt to bring the Church to the "Hebraic truth" of the Old Testament was fought by Augustine on the ground that the *Greek* translation of the Scriptures had been used in the past. Positions taken by Thomas Aquinas were regarded as dangerous innovations and departures from tradition by influential contemporaries of his day. Propositions held by Thomas along with others were condemned after his death by the Bishop of Paris.

This understanding of the irregular, spasmodic growth of theology in the past, with its accompanying hostile divisiveness, may enable us to grasp a little better the period of tremendous theological change in which we are living—a period when another tributary, that of knowledge flowing from recently developed sciences, pours its waters into the Christian mainstream of thought. Only those unaware of great theological changes in the past will be astounded by theological changes in the present. And it is no surprise that the present theological changes are once more producing divisive results in the Catholic community. On the one side (and inevitably) there will be a naive enthusiasm as if the new scientific knowledge and methods had all the answers—an enthusiasm that mistakes the tributary for the mainstream. On the other side, and more dangerously, there is the equally inevitable rigid opposition to the new knowledge. Once more the simplistic arguments against change will be brought forward. To admit that there can be theological change is to say that the Church of the past was wrong. How can we learn new things about Jesus Christ two thousand years after he lived? Such arguments stem from the failure to recognize the *human* component in all past (as well as present) phrasings of God's revelation. God and Jesus have always been understood through the prism of human minds limited in what they can grasp by the interpretative skills of their times. A God described in Semitic categories was understood differently from a God described in Platonic categories. Yet neither the Semitic nor the Platonic insight was exhaustive, nor did they totally agree. And today a God looked at through a world view aware of developments in the physical and social sciences will be understood differently from a God reflected upon by a medieval mind dominated by Aristotelian categories.

If one gives proper emphasis to the different human components in man's seeking to know God down through the ages, then it does not make sense to ask why the past did not formulate theology the way we do, when we have at our disposal a body of knowledge that was not available to the past. The fairest way of judging Christian theological endeavors of the past is on the basis of whether or not they used the knowledge at their disposal. And we Christians of today are liable to be judged harshly by the future if we do not use the new knowledge at our disposal in reflecting upon God. Those voices of the extreme right that want us to turn our back on all modern theological development would have the effect of reducing the

Church to a small sect frightened by the times in which it lives and seeking refuge in the past. The larger Christian vision is that, if there is new knowledge, we can use it to understand God anew, because knowledge that is true can always be put to the service of truth.

Development of Catholic Biblical Criticism

I have spoken in broad terms of new knowledge, stemming from a scientific mode of thought, that has been influencing contemporary theological insights. Let me illustrate this for you from the theological field I know best: Catholic biblical studies in the twentieth century.

Physical, historical, and linguistic methods, known to us only in approximately the last one hundred years, have produced a scientifically critical study of the Bible, a study that has revolutionized views held in the past about the authorship, origin, and dating of the biblical books, about how they were composed, and about what their authors meant. In the first forty years of this century (1900 to 1940 approximately) the Roman Catholic Church very clearly and officially took a stance against such biblical criticism. The Modernist heretics at the beginning of the century employed biblical criticism, and the official Roman condemnations of Modernism made little distinction between the possible intrinsic validity of biblical criticism and the theological misuse of it by the Modernists. Between 1905 and 1915 the Pontifical Biblical Commission in Rome issued a series of conservative decisions on the composition and authorship of the Bible. Although phrased with nuance, these decisions ran against the trends of contemporary Old and New Testament investigation. Yet Catholic scholars were obliged to assent to these decisions and to teach them.

After forty years of rigorous opposition, the Catholic Church in the 1940's under the pontificate of Pope Pius XII made an undeniable about-face in attitude toward biblical criticism. The encyclical *Divino Afflante Spiritu* (1943) instructed Catholic scholars to use the methods of a scientific approach to the Bible that had hitherto been forbidden to them. Within about ten years teachers trained in biblical criticism began to move in large numbers into Catholic classrooms in seminaries and colleges, so that the mid-1950's really marked the watershed. By that time the pursuit of the scientific method had led Catholic exegetes to abandon almost all the positions on biblical authorship and composition taken by Rome at the beginning of the century. No longer did they hold that Moses was the substantial author of the Pentateuch, that the first chapters of Genesis were really historical, that Isaiah was one book, that Matthew was the first Gospel written by an eyewitness, that Luke and Acts were written in the 60's, that Paul wrote Hebrews, etc. This dramatic change of position was tacitly acknowledged in 1955 by the secretary of the Pontifical Biblical Commission who stated that now Catholic scholars had *"complete freedom"* with regard to those decrees of 1905-1915 except where they touched on faith or morals (and very few of them did).[2]

Obviously this turn-about was not without opposition and anguish. Inevitably, clergy and religious who had been trained according to the earlier anti-critical positions were appalled at hearing a new generation of Catholics now teaching the very ideas they had been taught to consider as wrong and even heretical. But, in general, the change sparked a renewed interest in the Bible, indeed the greatest flowering of biblical study and writing that the Roman Catholic Church had ever seen. And so, wisely, the Church did not reverse the direction taken by Pius XII, despite the objections of those who were opposed to it. Rather his ideas on the Bible became part of the final schema on Revelation *(Dei Verbum)* of Vatican II.

In fact, the Church pushed on beyond the positions of Pius XII. The 1964 Pontifical Biblical Commission's *Instruction on the Historical Truth of the Gospels* dealt frankly with the delicate question of how accurately the Gospels report the words and deeds of Jesus. Much to the delight of Catholic biblical critics, the Commission made clear to Catholics that the Gospels are *not* literal, chronological accounts of the words and deeds of Jesus but are the product of a development through years of preaching, selection, synthesizing and explication. And, as a further sign of the Church's commitment to biblical criticism, in

---

[2]This statement and the Instruction of the Biblical Commission mentioned in a subsequent paragraph are reproduced in the Appendix of this book.

1972 Pope Paul VI restructured the Pontifical Biblical Commission so that scholars, instead of being merely consultors, now constituted the Commission itself. Those scholars whom he named were, in several instances, men who had suffered in the long battle to get biblical criticism accepted (David Stanley and Stanislaus Lyonnet); and the new secretary of the Commission, Bishop Descamps of Louvain, was a pioneer among Catholics in applying critical analysis to the resurrection narratives of the Gospels. All those appointed were men dedicated to the scientific approach to the Bible that is perfectly consonant with the best in Catholicism—men who would never have us go back to the fearful spirit that governed the dark days at the beginning of this century.

Impact on Theology of Other Disciplines

In the history I have given you, I have told you how for the first forty years of the century the Roman Catholic Church rejected biblical criticism and then how in the next thirty years it came to accept much of that criticism. That brings us up to the 1970's and the last third of the century. I venture to predict that this period into which we are now entering will be taken up with the impact of biblical criticism on the Roman Catholic understanding of doctrine. But before I show why this is likely to come about, let me give a reminder that in talking about our growth in biblical knowledge, I have chosen only one example of the new knowledge that has been put at the service of theology in our times. Many other examples might be cited. If there has been a development of our scientific knowledge of the history of biblical times, the same may be said of our knowledge of the history of Christianity. An older pattern of uniform development with occasional heretical deviations is no longer tenable, and we have come to recognize that pluralism existed since the earliest days. As we reread today the records of Church disputes, and of the Councils called to repudiate errors, we realize how the theology books of the last centuries have oversimplified the doctrinal conclusions based on such records. If we turn to moral or ethical theology, the availability of scientific psychology, sociology, and anthropology has challenged our generalizations about human behavior and its motives and the patterns of "natural law."

We may think too of the impact of ecumenism. Once more, for the first part of this century, the Roman Catholic Church was very apprehensive of world and regional ecumenical movements. Then suddenly, with Vatican II we embraced ecumenism with fervor. Dialogue group after dialogue group among the churches has been re-examining some of the most divisive questions of Christian theology and developing stances acceptable to both sides. Before 1965 it was virtually forbidden for Catholic students of theology to read the books of Protestant theologians and commentators without obtaining special permission or assurance that they were "safe." Now, I would guess, students in Catholic theology courses read as many non-Catholic works as Catholic ones. Obviously this broad reading, along with the presence of Protestant teachers in many Catholic institutions, brings new knowledge into the Catholic perspective.

And so in many fields besides the biblical, the knowledge explosion of our times is offering raw material for contemporary theological reflection. Yet, in a certain way this abundance of riches comes at a time when Catholic theology is not totally prepared to receive it. The years from 1700 to 1950 will probably be judged as a less productive period of Catholic thought, and indeed as a time when many attitudes were created that cause us difficulty today. Frightened by the upheavals of the Reformation, Catholic thinkers, of necessity, became apologetic in outlook—"apologetic" in the sense of defending past positions against the innovations of the Reformers. Authority was more and more centralized in Rome in order to prevent further Protestant inroads; and often Catholic theological positions were established by Roman condemnations of dangerous ideas, with theologians left only to supply arguments for what was already decided. Frequently leadership and direction in Catholic theology came from papal encyclicals and pronouncements and the decrees of the Roman Congregations. One may object to this picture by citing the names of a Newman or a Scheeben or the Catholic Tübingen school, but the sparsity of such names in a period of 250 years is itself an attestation that theological thought was coming from the top down and not from the bottom up. The net result of all this is that we have become unaccustomed to theological innovation and tend to look on it askance, as if it were a usurpation to have theologians thinking for themselves.

Historical Limitations of Dogma

However, if this general attitude that theology should "follow the leader" is an obstacle to the impact of the contemporary knowledge explosion on Catholic theology, there are other factors which will heighten the impact. If I may return to the biblical field, biblical criticism can have an enormous effect on theology precisely because the Second Vatican Council raised biblical exegesis from the status of second-class citizenship to which it had been reduced among Catholics by an overreaction to the Protestant claim for its autonomy. The Council (*Dei Verbum* ii 9) stated that "Sacred Tradition and Sacred Scripture are to be accepted and venerated with the same sense of devotion and reverence." The living teaching office of the Church "is not above the word of God but serves it" and must listen to the word devoutly as part of the process of interpreting it (ii 10). The model, then, is not one of autonomy, either of Tradition over scriptural interpretation (the popular Catholic model of post-reformation times) or of scriptural interpretation over Church Tradition (a popular understanding of the Protestant position); the model is one of mutual influence. And this mutual influence will inevitably involve tension when one serves to modify the other in promoting the Church's grasp of God's truth.

The possibility that biblical and other knowledge may modify Tradition is heightened by another insight that has become respectable in Catholic circles in the aftermath of Vatican II. In the speech with which he opened the Council (Oct. 11, 1962) Pope John XXIII made one of the most important magisterial admissions of modern times: "The substance of the ancient doctrine of the deposit of faith is one thing, and the way in which it is presented is another." In other words the Pope opened the possibility of distinguishing between a revealed doctrine and the way in which it has been formulated. The key to biblical criticism was the recognition that, while the Scriptures are the word of God, they do not escape the limitations of history. Rather the Scriptures reflect the limited views current in specific periods of human history, and this historical context must be taken into account in interpreting the weight and import of their inspired message. And now the Pope's statement led many to the conclusion that the doctrinal statements of the Church were under a similar historical limitation. While doctrinal formulations of the past capture an aspect of revealed truth, they do not exhaust it; they represent the limited insight of one period of Church history which can be *modified* in another period of Church history as Christians approach the truth from a different direction or with new tools of investigation.[3]

Notice that I said "modified," for the majority of Catholic theologians maintain that past insights are not wiped out by subsequent developments. For them, a truly Christian sense of tradition limits the possibilities of change. In other words, when theologians like Avery Dulles speak of "the historical relativity of all doctrinal statements" (*The Survival of Dogma*, p. 173), they are not rejecting the infallibility of past dogmas but are seeking to sharpen our understanding of the range of infallibility against an over-simplified concept that removes doctrinal statements from all limitations of space and time. Very often the "modification" that modern theological speculation makes possible is in bringing the Church to distinguish between those elements of previous formulations which are permanently helpful and those elements which are so time-conditioned that they

---

[3]Subsequently, my remarks here about the historical limitations of doctrinal statements and my insistence that theological reflection has shaped dogmatic formulations (see the second section of the address) were vigorously attacked by the ultra-conservative Catholic press which seemed to maintain that God Himself directly revealed doctrinal formulations and that they did not come from men and so were not changeable. But within three months of the time I gave this address the Roman Doctrinal Congregation (former Holy Office) issued *Mysterium Ecclesiae*, a pertinent section of which I quote in the Appendix. It eloquently confirms my contention that, while dogmas really capture an aspect of the truth (and so are not indeterminate expressions to be relativized away), they express that truth in a historically conditioned and limited way which may need rephrasing, ultimately to be approved by the Church.

can best be dispensed with. By way of example, the physical sciences have traced patterns of human evolution; biblical criticism has given a better understanding of the type of literature represented by the early chapters of Genesis; and so together the physical sciences and biblical criticism have helped Catholics to see that in the ancient doctrine of God's creation of man it is *no longer necessary* to maintain that man's body was directly created by God from the earth, or that woman's body was directly created from man's. In times past such a direct creation of the body would have been considered part of the doctrine; today we continue to maintain the doctrine of creation without trying to rule out the possibility of evolution.

Role of the Magisterium

In this whole process wherein modern knowledge *contributes* toward reformulation or modification of ancient doctrine, the key word is "contribute." No theologians, no matter how impressive their evidence, can formulate Catholic doctrines. They can only make a contribution that must be assessed in the wider context of the Church's life guided by the Spirit. They can put their evidence at the service of the official magisterium which often by a tolerance of new theological views acknowledges the impact of the opinions of theologians. Thus, in the instance I cited, it would be foolish for us to expect that Catholic Church authorities will pronounce that man's body has evolved from a lower animal form—that is a question of science—but the fact that Catholic theologians are allowed to teach the possibility of evolution represents a change in the Catholic position.

The cooperation between theologians and the official magisterium of Pope and Bishops remains absolutely essential in a time of polarization toward extremes. I have pointed out that there is no major tendency among Catholic theologians to reject in any casual manner the doctrines of the past, but only to recognize their limitations; similarly there is no major tendency to usurp the authority of the magisterium and to pretend that theologians can formulate doctrine. On the other hand the positive attitude of the magisterium toward modern biblical studies and modern theology has been very beneficial, precisely in preventing an exaggerated swing to the left.

The continued support of the magisterium is all the more necessary now that a danger both to theology and magisterium has arisen on the right. With increasing frequency ultra-conservative or fundamentalist Catholics are usurping the authority of the magisterium by trying to condemn as heretical all theological speculation that shows any sign of nuance with regard to past doctrine. They do not respect the positions of the Popes or the Bishops who have permitted modern biblical and theological advances; rather these Catholic fundamentalists denounce as heretical the freer Catholic positions that have emerged from Vatican II. It is no accident that in the last six months several prominent American Cardinals have had to denounce the irresponsibility of the arch-conservative sector of the Catholic press with its very negative attitude toward modern developments in the Church. And, we may note, in theological questions journalistic abuse is often the only road open to such Catholic fundamentalists; for their opinions have little or no scholarly respectability, and so Catholic colleges and universities and reputable Catholic scholarly periodicals will give them no voice. Despite the annoyance caused by these arch-conservatives, our great assurance for the future is that the real organs of Catholic theological education are solidly in the hands of those who accept reasonable modern insights.

Nevertheless, in face of this tendency of right-wing vigilantes to pretend to be able to speak for Catholicism when they attack every new idea, it is important that the Bishops support the legitimacy and the rights of responsible Catholic theological investigation, so that it will be clear in the minds of the Catholic people that there is nothing unCatholic about studying the theological problems that have arisen in our time. We must dispel once and for all the fundamentalist supposition that a theologian is more loyal to the Church if he does not recognize that a difficult problem exists. The trust between theologians and Bishops that arose at Vatican II led to great progress in the Church; and theologians must take care on their part not to let that trust be eroded. They must make it apparent to the Bishops that there is no danger to the Church from responsible modern theological reflection, no matter how sensitive the areas it probes. The real danger is from those ultra-liberals who scorn serious theology and from those ultra-conservatives who see in every investigation a threat to faith.

THE EFFECT ON THE TEACHING OF CATHOLIC DOCTRINE

Thus far I have been attempting to explain why we are in a time of theological change so acute that it may be called a crisis. We have become conscious that all human formulations of truth are limited, and in the light of vast new bodies of knowledge we are attempting to rethink past understandings of divine truth to see if enriching new insights and modifications are possible. But in such a time of change, how do we communicate Catholic doctrine to new generations of Christians? Because theologians are rethinking aspects of past doctrines, are teachers of doctrine to become tongue-tied as if there were nothing certain that they could pass on?—as if everything doctrinal were "up-for-grabs"? Personally I can think of no greater disaster for Catholicism.

But before I face directly the problem of the communication of doctrine in a time of theological change, let me comment on a rather simplistic way of attempting to solve the problem. I refer to a misunderstanding of the distinction between "faith" and "theology." We cannot answer our problem fully by stating that in catechetics teachers are communicating Catholic faith *independently* of theological disputation. When "faith" is used in such a statement, what is generally meant is the content of belief—the formulations of faith, the dogmas, the doctrines. But such a sharp distinction between the formulations of our faith and theological discussions may give the erroneous impression that such formulations were not the product of theology, as man reflected upon his God, but rather came down ready-made from heaven. This is simply not so (see footnote 3). *Every formulation that we accept as part of the contents of our faith is the product of theological reflection.*

While God has revealed Himself in creation and in history (particularly in the history of Israel and in the life of Jesus and his Church), He has not directly revealed a body of formulas.

The vocalizing of revelation, the development of the formulas that capture for each age necessary insights into revelation, is achieved by God's guiding *men* in their understanding and reflection to a grasp of truth. God has also guided His Church to recognize formulas that are more adequate than others to express divine truth (and, in addition, to reject some formulas as inadequate or false). Consequently, the distinction between (the formulas of) "faith" and "theology" is really a distinction between *theological formulas that the Church has made her own* by declaring that they reflect divine truth and *theological formulas to which the Church has made no formal commitment.* By emphasizing the fact that theological reflection is involved in both (the formulas of) "faith" and "theology," we see that it is too simple to say: Teach the faith and forget about theology. This is especially true today since modern theological discussion is not focused on marginal questions but on a contemporary reunderstanding of the *fundamental* teachings of Christianity.

If teachers cannot facilely ignore theological discussion when they are communicating the formulas of faith, how then do we avoid having catechetics reduced to uncertainties? It is here that our understanding of the *validity* of past formulations plays a role. Precisely because past formulations reflect a *valid* if limited grasp of divine truth, we can use those formulations, provided that we are aware of both their validity and their limitations. As a good, practical example of this, let us turn our attention to the January 1973 publication by the American Bishops of the *Basic Teachings for Catholic Religious Education.*

First of all, the Bishops have taken an admirable step in insuring that our catechetics should communicate content as well as attitude. It may be true that in the past we were too content-oriented in catechetics, too interested in formulas rather than in formation of Christian character. But it is also true that there has been recently a danger of over-reaction in the other direction, as if the learning of formulas and prayers were not part of Christian education. In a catechetical period that is laudably interested in formation, the Bishops have insured that the ancient content of our faith is not forgotten.

Second, the Bishops have expressed their *Basic Teachings*

in a way that shows a sensitivity about both the validity and the limitations of past conceptions of doctrine. They cover the necessary span of Christian teaching: the Triune God; His creation; Jesus, true God and true man; the incarnation and resurrection; the sacraments and the Church; man and his freedom; his sin, original and personal, and his morality; and finally the Virgin Mary, the Mother of God and the model of the Church —in short, all that we Christians should consider the authentic teachings of the faith. Yet, as far as I can see, the Bishops have taken care *not* to include in the formulations of these ancient doctrines phrasings that would hinder the legitimate discussions of modern theology.

Let me give some examples. The Bishops have spoken of God's creation of the world, but there is not a word against evolution and no indication that the Genesis account of creation must be taken literally. The Bishops speak about the humanity of Jesus, mentioning the only difference that Scripture and the Council of Chalcedon make between his humanity and ours: he is like us in everything *except sin*. The Bishops wisely stress that he is "the perfect man," which means that he has all the perfections that men have—but they never attribute to his humanity perfections that do not belong to men, for instance, omniscience. Thus there is nothing in the Bishops' document contrary to modern biblical and theological speculation which takes the limitations of Jesus' human knowledge very seriously.[4] Again, the Bishops state that "by God's design the Church is a society with leaders, i.e., with a hierarchy," but they do not get into the disputed theological question of whether the hierarchy stems from the historical Jesus or whether it was developed under the guidance of the Spirit.

I could give many more examples showing the subtlety of the Bishops' document and their care not to cause conflict with genuine theological interests. I emphasize this because, in our polarized Church, liberals may have a tendency to dismiss carelessly the Bishops' *Basic Teachings* as old-fashioned and too content-oriented. This is to play into the hands of arch-conser-

---

[4]See footnote 27, below in Chapter Two.

vatives who will be only too happy to monopolize this document and interpret it as a condemnation of modern theology. Indeed, the very week that the Bishops approved the document, there appeared in the Catholic right-wing press the claim that the Bishops had contradicted new theology at almost every point.

I have said above that the arch-conservative section of the Catholic press has usurped the authority of the Church's magisterium to judge what is orthodox in theology—these propagandists think they can condemn theologians as heretical. But more seriously they are trying to usurp the Bishops' authority to determine what can be taught as Catholic doctrine to the youth. They do not hesitate to denounce catechisms approved by the Bishops with an incredible demand to return to the Baltimore Catechism. Often they seek to set up their own catechetical schools to seal off the youth from any contact with ideas more enlightened than their own and thus to divide this group of Catholic youth from their confreres who attend the regular catechetical instruction. And now they will have the arrogance to impose on the Bishops' *Basic Teachings* their own interpretations that go beyond what the Bishops have said and to use these interpretations to frustrate the freedom the Bishops have allowed. These voices from the extreme right are alienated and unhappy voices in the Roman Catholic Church today—that is a tragedy that I wish with all my heart could have been avoided. But it will be a greater tragedy if through a manipulation of catechetics which tries to turn the clock back on genuine Catholic theological progress, they succeed in creating a future generation of youth that will be even less at home in the Catholic movements of this century than their parents are.[5]

An effective way for teachers of Catholic doctrine to com-

---

[5]On the basis of this paragraph it has been falsely charged that in this address I attempted to deny parents any voice in the religious education of their children. My paragraph is clearly directed not against parents but against "the arch-conservative section of the Catholic press" and the organized pressure groups that press has spawned which attempt to constitute themselves the arbiter of what shall be taught *in catechisms* to Catholic children. The claim that I was infringing on the rights of ordinary parents to guide their children is a red herring.

bat this divisive tendency is to follow the lead the Bishops have given us. Teachers should present in catechetics the fundamentals the Bishops have underscored in their document, and yet at the same time pedagogically prepare the students for a future encounter with theological discussions about aspects of doctrine that the Bishops have left open. For instance, we should teach the students the doctrine of original sin, and we should point out that this doctrine has been phrased in terms of the Adam and Eve story of Genesis (a story with which students should be made familiar). But we should stress that the Genesis story is only a vehicle for the doctrine of original sin and not the substance of the teaching. Moreover, in loyalty to modern biblical scholarship, we should point out that the Genesis story is not an exact historical account of the origins of man. Thereby we prepare students for the possibility that, under the impact of theological reflection, the Church may not always phrase the doctrine of original sin in terms of a sin committed by Adam and Eve as sole parents of the human race.

In conclusion, the kind of teaching I am suggesting requires a double effort: an effort to examine with precision the basic doctrines of our faith, such as those listed by the Bishops; and an effort to keep abreast of modern theological discussion, so that the limitations of past understandings of those doctrines are not imposed on the students as if they had to be believed. The Bishops have made clear their desire that teachers should not impose on students modern theological reflections as if they were doctrine, but that does not mean that teachers should not prepare the students for the effects of modern theological discussions. Nor does it mean that teachers can impose on students discredited or dubious theological reflections of the past simply because it causes less disturbance to parents. In the long run, a failure to prepare the students for modern insights into the limitations of our past understandings of truth equips a student poorly to face the world in which he or she will live. It is a dangerous invitation to a loss of faith through confusion.

Let us have the courage, then, to present our doctrines with an appreciation of their greatness; yet at the same time to prepare our students to survive in an age of theological change. It is a challenge, but a challenge that stems from a period of great

Christian vitality. After several rather barren centuries in the history of Catholic theological thought, we have come alive again theologically. Let those who are afraid of the changes of our times condemn them; *our* task is to capitalize on the opportunity of our time to preach with joy the Good News of our faith in what God has done, not only what He has done in the past, but what He is doing today as well.

A respect for the past and an openness to the present are what I am urging. And in doing so I trust I am meeting the real concern and theme of this convention: RELIGIOUS EDUCATION: BUILDING VALUES AND MEANING. The recognition and communication of the valid insights in past doctrinal formulations *builds values*. An openness to present insights and to what God has enabled us to see anew about His revelation in our times *gives meaning*. To neglect either the heritage of the past or the contribution of the present is a failure in *religious education*.

2.
"Who Do Men Say That I Am?"— A Survey of Modern Scholarship on Gospel Christology[6]

I trust that my choice of the topic of christology for an address to a national convention of the College Theology Society needs no explanation. Christology was, is, and, I suspect, always will be the single most important question in Christian theology. Of the three religions of the book, Judaism, Christianity, and Islam, we Christians are the only ones who have accepted identification in terms of our stance about a person of history, Jesus of Nazareth. Although Judaism reveres Moses as the lawgiver, the designation "Judaism" suggests that primary identity is not in terms of an attitude toward Moses but in terms of relationship to the tribe of Judah and the people of Israel. Westerners persist in calling Muslims "Mohammedans," but that is by false analogy with the title "Christians." While Mohammed is *the* prophet, a Muslim is one who has accepted Islam, that is, submission to the will of Allah, as preached by Mohammed. Christians, however, are those who profess that Jesus of Nazareth is the Messiah, the Christ. The question "Who do men say that I am?" stands in a central place in the tradition of the Synoptic Gospels, symptomatic of where it stands in our faith; and we Christians are those who think that,

---

[6]An address to the June 1974 national convention of the College Theology Society at the University of Dayton (and reported in *Horizons*, the journal of that Society [Fall, 1974 issue]). It is reproduced here with minor changes.

whether he understood it fully or not, Peter gave the correct answer to that question.[7]

I am going to speak here of one aspect of christology, the christology of the New Testament, and particularly of the Gospels. While, in a literal sense, christology involves the evaluation of Jesus as the Christ (Messiah), I shall use it in the customary wider sense of any traditional evaluation of Jesus, e.g., in the NT area, the evaluations of him as the Servant of God, the Prophet, the Lord, the Son of Man, the Son of God, and even God. Such evaluations are found in NT works written anywhere from twenty to one hundred years after the ministry of Jesus,[8] and the particular point to which I direct this paper is: How are these NT evaluations of Jesus related to the earlier evaluation of Jesus during the ministry? Did Jesus himself use these titles? Did he accept them if others applied them to him? If not, how did he evaluate himself?

In discussing the relationship of the christology of Jesus' ministry to the christology of the NT writings, I shall present a survey of scholarly and non-scholarly views on the problem. I use the term "non-scholarly" without prejudice to designate views that are not held by reputable scholars writing in the field today.[9] Actually, as we shall see, non-scholarly views have a

---

[7]As will be pointed out, the answer given in Mark's account is different from the answer given in Matthew's account, but both agree that Peter acknowledged Jesus as Messiah. I do not accept the view that the Marcan Peter is made the spokesman of an erroneous christology which Mark is trying to correct; rather, in Mark Peter is the spokesman of an inadequate christology (see the treatment of Peter in Mark in Chapter Four below).

[8]The first NT work was I Thessalonians, written about A.D. 50. The last NT work was probably II Peter written in the first half of the second century. Give or take ten years, the Gospels may be plausibly dated as follows: Mark in the late 60's; Matthew and Luke in the 80's; John in the 90's.

[9]In my outlook reputable scholars are those who have produced a body of articles that meet the publishing standards of the professional biblical journals, or whose books have been favorably reviewed in such journals. Thus, I am not speaking simply about those who have biblical degrees or who teach Bible. I find it necessary to be precise here because, on the American Catholic scene in the last two years, fundamentalist newspapers and journals have had a habit of trotting out a polemicist, dubbing him a scholar, and then playing a game of "scholars are divided" in order to propose views that have no serious following in the world of biblical scholarship.

TWENTIETH-CENTURY VIEWS ON THE CHRISTOLOGY OF THE NEW TESTAMENT

(A survey of opinions on the relationship between the evaluation of Jesus during his ministry and the christological evaluation of him in the NT writings composed some twenty to one hundred years later.)

NON-SCHOLARLY LIBERALISM	VIEWS WITHIN THE DOMAIN OF SCHOLARSHIP			NON-SCHOLARLY CONSERVATISM
	SCHOLARLY LIBERALISM	BULTMANNIAN EXISTENTIALISM	MODERATE CONSERVATISM	
This view regards the christological question as unimportant, for Christianity is primarily concerned with how man should live. Jesus came to teach man a way of life centered on love. It was his followers who first gave any importance to evaluating him. Liberalism was popular in the Protestantism of the late 1800's and early 1900's. It has revived today in Catholicism as a reaction to the dogmatic strictness of the past.	(Early 1900's) Liberal scholars developed a scientific methodology for detecting precise stages of growth in NT christology. They judged this growth to be a creation, distorting the historical Jesus. Christology was once necessary in order to preserve the memory of Jesus, but now modern scholarship can give us the historical Jesus without christology, which should be dispensed with. Exemplified in W. Bousset's *Kyrios Christos* (1913).	(1920's through the 1950's) A reaction to liberalism. He further refined the scientific methodology, but rejected the liberal judgment on the invalidity of christology. Bultmann is indefinite and even agnostic on how Jesus evaluated himself. But the NT christology is functionally equivalent to Jesus' message about the kingdom, since both are a demand to accept what God has done through Jesus. Christology cannot be dispensed with.	(1960's and 1970's) Most scholars today are less agnostic than Bultmann about the historical Jesus and admit a continuity between the evaluation of Jesus during the ministry and the evaluation of him in the NT. Yet they continue to use with refinement the methodology for detecting growth in NT christology. The dominating motif is development in continuity. A division exists as to whether to posit an explicit christology in the ministry of Jesus (he used or accepted some titles: Son of Man, Suffering Servant, Messiah) or an implicit christology (Jesus did not use or accept christological titles). IMPLICIT CHRISTOLOGY / EXPLICIT CHRISTOLOGY Scholars such as Hahn, Fuller, Perrin; some post-Bultmannians; many Catholics of the 1970's. Scholars such as Cullmann, Jeremias, Dodd, Taylor; most Catholics of the 1960's.	A failure to allow any development from the ministry to the NT. This theory posits that Jesus was christologically evaluated during his ministry exactly as he is portrayed in the Gospels (which are literal accounts of the ministry). A view held defensively by fundamentalist Protestants. Also held by Catholics until Church changes in the approach to the Bible began to affect Gospel study in the 1960's.

wider following than scholarly views have, and for that reason we must be aware of them when we teach. In presenting the scholarly views, I am not pretending to offer anything startlingly new;[10] rather I am showing you how one might organize chronologically and classify the results of twentieth-century scholarship pertaining to NT christology. I am hoping that this may be of use to you pedagogically and, indeed, even pastorally since misunderstandings over christology are a very divisive force in Christianity today.[11]

As you can see from the accompanying chart, I divide the scholarly and non-scholarly views into six categories, represented by columns. I admit from the start that such a categorization oversimplifies and does at least minor injustice. Therefore, if you have occasion to use these reflections in your own teaching, I invite you to introduce greater precision than is possible for me in a one-hour talk. As part of the categorization I shall use the terms conservative and liberal. A conservative christological view, for me, is one that posits a *real* relationship between the christology of Jesus' ministry (or his self-evaluation) and the christology of the NT writings—a relationship that may run the gamut from identity to varying degrees of continuity. A liberal christological view is one that denies any real relationship or continuity between the evaluation of Jesus during his ministry and the way he was later preached by the Church.

To avert any guessing game as to which column I would place myself in, may I suggest a more fruitful approach to my exegetical Bingo card, namely, for you to determine in which column *you* belong.

---

[10]For this reason there will be no attempt to equip this paper with detailed footnotes giving bibliographical background. The history recounted and the biblical views presented can be documented in the standard NT introductions.

[11]I am presuming that many in the College Theology Society will share a pastoral concern for the Church and regard religion as more than simply a scientific discipline.

TWENTIETH-CENTURY VIEWS

Non-Scholarly Conservatism

Accepting the usual convention that right is conservative and left is liberal, let me begin with the column on the extreme right of my chart, namely, with a conservatism that lies outside the scope of respectable modern scholarship. This conservatism *identifies* the christology of the Gospels with the christology of Jesus. Even though the Gospels were written some thirty to sixty years after the ministry of Jesus, this conservatism maintains that there has been *no significant christological development*. For instance, if in the Gospel of Matthew, Jesus accepts enthusiastically Peter's confession that he is the Messiah, the Son of the living God, that acceptance reflects the self-evaluation of the historical Jesus—despite the fact that Peter's confession and Jesus' reaction are quite different in the earlier Gospel of Mark. If, in the Gospel of John, Jesus speaks as a pre-existent divine figure (8:58; 17:5), he actually spoke that way during his lifetime—despite the fact that there is no indication of that in the Synoptic tradition.

This rigorous conservative view would be held by many church-going Christians, but probably with a different tonality by Protestants and by Catholics. Protestants (and this would include fundamentalists, as well as some of the main-line Reformation churches south of the Mason-Dixon line) often hold this view defensively. They know that as a result of biblical criticism the major Reformation churches have for the most part adopted a nuanced view about the NT; they know that the major Protestant seminaries and theology schools teach biblical criticism; but they reject biblical criticism in favor of literalism. On the other hand, Catholics who are extremely conservative, even though very numerous in both the clergy and the laity, have not, at least up until the last few years, been defensive in biblical questions—the vast mass of Catholics were totally unaware that there was any view other than that the Gospels reproduced literally the ministry of Jesus. The condemnations of Modernism were so rigorously enforced in the years following 1910 that no real biblical criticism in the area of the NT was ever widely expounded in Catholic seminaries and universities, and so both priests and laity took it for granted that the Gospels were lives of Jesus. However, as we all know, an enormous change began in Catholic circles[12] with the papal encyclical *Divino Afflante Spiritu* (1943) and culminated in the Instruction of the Pontifical Biblical Commission *The Historical Truth of the Gospels* (1964).[13] In the latter document Catholics are told that the Gospels are the product of a three-stage development that involved many changes and that, therefore, the Gospels are not literal accounts of the words of Jesus. Moreover, the Biblical Commission stresses that the divinity of Jesus was not clearly perceived until after the resurrection. All of this teaches Catholics that there must have been a development of christology between the ministry of Jesus and the time the Gospels were written, and so rules out for Catholics an ultra-conservative approach.

This sudden change of teaching-position within Catholicism is inevitably going to produce a defensiveness among Catholics who persist in holding onto a literalistic approach to the Gospels. This defensiveness will be aggravated by the fact that the clergy ordained in the last ten years are being taught this thesis of Gospel development advocated by the Biblical Commission, a thesis which is directly opposite to the basic approach taught most of the clergy before the 1960's—with the result that the people often hear contradictory things about the Gospels from the pulpit, with the accompanying warning that the opposing view is, respectively, either "out of date" or "dangerously novel." It may well be that many priests trained before the 1960's have never heard of the 1964 Biblical Commission Instruction, and so do not know what the Church is now teaching about the Gospels, while those trained in and after the 1960's have little knowledge of the ultra-conservative views previously

---

[12]A more ample account of this change and development in Catholic biblical criticism appears in the address which constitutes the first chapter of this book. Here, however, I am particularly concerned with the application of biblical criticism to the NT and to the Gospels—the application to the OT came sooner. Even in the NT field we should note that in the first half of this century there were individual Catholic scholars who, sometimes confidentially, and more often in lectures than in writing, dared to challenge literal Gospel historicity.

[13]For this Instruction see the Appendix, especially the italicized passages.

taught in Catholic seminaries. But we should not despair. There is still time to bring clergy and laity to understand that the "new" look in Roman Catholic approaches to the Bible is not destructive of faith and indeed is more plausible historically, something they are in a position to understand because of historical development in religion in our own times. I say that there is still time to reach the mass of Catholics unless they are falsely alarmed and their minds poisoned by the hysterical propaganda of a militant Catholic fundamentalist movement. Because such a movement exists,[14] it is crucial that teachers of religion think of a wider audience than their own students.

For instance, we all know that it is relatively easy to bring open-minded college students to understand the positive possibilities of our modern biblical and theological approaches to christology. It is more difficult for the teacher to prepare them to share this understanding with parents and acquaintances, and even with clergy whose training and outlook are the non-scholarly conservatism I have been discussing. If students can be trained to communicate modern views with patience and explanation, they can greatly facilitate among Catholics a transition from a position that is no longer tenable. But if students are not taught to make allowance for the mindset of previous generations, they may appear as arrogant and skeptical and thus further the process of polarization in the Church. Above all, I would appeal to the College Teachers of Religion to counteract the fundamentalist ploy which insists that widely accepted modern views on christology should be kept in the classroom but not allowed to be communicated more broadly lest they disturb the faithful.[15] What is involved here are not "wild" views but views

---

[14]In the address which constitutes the first chapter of this book I spoke about a dangerous pseudo-magisterium consisting of extremist right-wing newspapers, magazines, and pressure groups that arrogate to themselves the right to designate as heretical or Modernist views and books approved by the true magisterium of pope and bishops. Although I mentioned by name no writer, newspaper, or journal, extremist organs and spokesmen in the United States hastened to identify themselves as the object of my remarks—a classic case of the shoe's fitting.

[15]It is commonsense that sometimes subjects are too complicated to be broached in short talks to an unprepared public and that exploratory views should be ex-

of a moderate growth in christology in harmony with the principles of Gospel development inculcated by Church documents. To claim that these views must be kept in the classroom is simply a technique of isolating the Church from its scholars who can then be portrayed as a snobbish and irreverent elite.

Non-Scholarly Liberalism

Instead of moving in my chart to the next column and thus from an extreme conservatism to a more moderate conservatism, I would like to jump to the other end of the spectrum, namely, to the liberal extreme which also lies outside the scope of modern scholarship. Such a jump is not illogical, for it is frequently made by right-wing Christians when they recognize the indefensibility of the rigid tenets they have hitherto held. The domino theory seems to prevail in religion whether or not it applies in global politics. If, through study, an extreme conservative comes to realize that the Gospels are not literal accounts of the ministry of Jesus and that there has been development, the reaction is often to ask not "How much development?" but "How do I know that any of it is true?" From the contention that the divinity of Jesus was not clearly perceived during his ministry, the next step of literal-minded people is sometimes to conclude that therefore Jesus was nothing more than an ordinary man, except that he was more brilliant and more "charismatic." Such an attitude means that there is *no continuity* between Jesus' self-evaluation and the exalted christological

---

amined before wide dissemination. But it is quite different to pretend that what is taught in seminary and college classrooms is too dangerous or disturbing to be made known to the faithful. Modern biblical and theological views are time-conditioned and have an element of uncertainty, but that is no excuse for pretending that they can be ignored until some mythical future day when absolute certainty is possible. No greater certitude should be demanded of biblical criticism or of theology today than was demanded in the past when there were formulated the very views that ultra-conservatives would like to hold onto. The contrast is not, as some would have it, between past Catholic doctrine and modern scholarly opinion; the contrast is between past scholarly opinion accepted within Catholicism and modern scholarly opinion now finding acceptance within Catholicism. Unfortunately a naive understanding of the scope and effect of infallibility blinds many to the *fact* that Catholicism has frequently adopted scholarly opinions that it later rejected.

evaluations of him found in the NT documents.

The non-scholarly aspect of this liberalism is its dismissal of the christology of the NT as unimportant. Already in the late eighteenth century there were attempts to eliminate the doctrinal sections of the NT and so to preserve just the moral injunctions of Jesus and of Paul. Today a broad christological liberalism sometimes appears in the "Christianity is love" discoveries.[16] There is nothing wrong in that statement when love is understood as the *agapē* lauded by Paul and John—a highly christological understanding of love which involves a judgment about Jesus as the Son of God. But the modern exponent of "Christianity is love" may be thinking much more in terms of self-fulfillment. The slogan may spring from an understanding of religion as a matter of the way one lives, no matter what one believes. I do not mean to devalue the meaningfulness of self-fulfillment or of the necessity of translating religion into practice; but I do not think that love, so understood, is an adequate definition of Christianity, for it can be found in other religions and among the non-religious. If it is true that there can be no Christianity without love, Christians remain those who base their love on a confession about Jesus. Every NT proclamation of the Gospel involves an evaluation of Jesus, his person and his ministry.

Scholarly Liberalism

Leaving aside the two extreme views, I would now like to

---

[16]Ironically, this may be more of a danger among Catholics than among Protestants today. Protestantism went through a major struggle with liberalism at the beginning of this century and suffered its losses then. But in the wake of Vatican II, as a reaction to exaggerated dogmatism, contemporary "liberated" Catholics have sometimes thrown aside all doctrinal content for an experiential grasp of religion. The reaction to a catechetics than overly stressed content and memory has sometimes been a total neglect of content and memory. If in the long run one must evaluate the danger presented by the two extremes, namely an ultra-conservatism and a doctrine-free liberalism, one must remember that the ultra-conservatives have money, organization, and fanatical persistence on their side. Liberalism by its very nature tends to be disorganized and ephemeral. The ultra-liberal press has either gone under or been tamed; ultra-conservatives have been buying up journals of opinion. Ultra-liberalism may well be a greater distortion of truth than ultra-conservatism, but it is much less likely to survive.

turn to christologies that lie within the pale of scholarship. De-
signating them as "scholarly" does not mean that I think they
are necessarily convincing in their argumentation; it means simply that reputable scholars hold them.[17] Let me begin by calling
attention to a liberalism that has such a scholarly basis.

Scholarly liberalism differs from non-scholarly liberalism
in several important ways. It does not dismiss the christology of
the NT as unimportant. It recognizes that that NT is shot
through with christology from beginning to end and that its authors claimed far more than that Christianity was a morality.
Yet it is designated as liberalism because it regards the christology of the NT as a mistaken evaluation of Jesus which does not
stand in real continuity with the self-evaluation of Jesus. For the
liberals, the christology of the NT is a creation, nay, a *creatio
ex nihilo*; and scholarly liberals have sought to trace this cre-
ative process by a careful methodology.

All scholars must admit that it was the liberals who worked
out a detailed schema of the growth of thought in early Christian communities. Through their efforts we became aware of the
possibility of distinctive theological viewpoints proper to the
Palestinian communities of Aramaic/Hebrew-speaking Jewish
Christians, to the Syrian communities of Greek-speaking Jewish
Christians, to the Greek-speaking Gentile Christians of the
churches of Asia Minor and Greece, and finally to communities
influenced by individual geniuses such as Paul and John. Only
in the past century has scholarship had the linguistic and historical data necessary for detecting such phases of Christian
thought. For instance, although previous scholarship had known
Aramaic, the main bodies of comparative Aramaic literature
came from several centuries before Jesus (Imperial Aramaic) or
from several centuries after Jesus (Syriac and Talmudic Aramaic). To reconstruct the language of Jesus from such evidence
was not unlike trying to reconstruct Shakespearian English
from Chaucer and the *New York Times*. But increasingly in the
last one hundred years there has become available a body of
Aramaic (and of Hebrew) dating from the time of Jesus. Moreover, with the discovery of documents like the Dead Sea Scrolls

---

[17]See footnote 9 above.

we have gained a more accurate picture of the pluralistic Judaism of Jesus' time, instead of having to reconstruct the entire situation from the Pharisaic-rabbinic documents of later centuries. These discoveries, plus a sharper application of a comparative criticism of inter-Gospel relationships, have confirmed the basic methodology of the liberal scholars who flourished in the early 1900's, although some of their simplified schematizations have been qualified.[18]

However, the liberals' methodological plotting of the development of christology is one thing; their value-judgment on that development is another thing. For instance, it may be correct to observe that the title "Lord" reflected a higher christology when applied to Jesus in a Greek-speaking Jewish community as *Kyrios* than when applied to him in an Aramaic-speaking community as *Mārè*. The prayer *Maranatha* assures us that Jesus was called "Lord" by early Aramaic-speaking Christians, but we have no evidence that the title carried the same theological "freight" as *Kyrios* which seemingly was used by Greek-speaking Jews to render the tetragrammaton YHWH.[19] If the use of *Kyrios* for Jesus carried overtones of the sphere of divinity, how is one to evaluate such a development of meaning? Scholarly methodology enables one to recognize the development but does not settle the question of whether such a development was a falsification or a deeper perception.

Many of the liberal scholars who wrote before World War I[20] assumed that the newfound ability to trace the development

---

[18]The chief qualification comes from an increasing uncertainty about the ability to regard Hellenistic (Greek) features in the christology as coming from the later levels of the NT. The Palestine of Jesus' time was thoroughly Hellenized, and some Hellenization of the Christian message may have been a feature from the very beginning. Moreover, we have become aware that various stages of the development may have coexisted, so that the process was much less linear than was formerly imagined.

[19]We must be cautious here and recognize the tentative nature of scholarly conclusions. In *New Testament Studies* 20 (1973-74), 388-90, J. A. Fitzmyer has shown from Dead Sea Scroll Aramaic that *mārè* can be used absolutely as "the Lord" and be a name for God, even though the Aramaic usage is not completely parallel to the Greek *Kyrios*.

[20]Perhaps the best example of scholarly liberalism both as to method and to conclusions was Wilhelm Bousset, *Kyrios Christos*. The German original ap-

of a higher christology indicated that a divine image had been created for Jesus. In their minds this invented christology was a *felix culpa* because only through such divinization was the memory of Jesus preserved. The historical Jesus was a preacher of stark ethical demand who challenged the religious institutions and cut through the false ideas of his time. His ideals and insights were not lost because the community imposed on its memory of him a christology and turned him into the heavenly Son of Man, the Lord and Judge of the world, indeed into the Son of God. But if in centuries past such a christological crutch was necessary to keep the memory of Jesus operative, in the judgment of the liberal scholars the crutch could now be discarded. Twentieth-century scholarship could detect the real Jesus and hold onto him without the christological trappings. Thus the ultimate implication of scholarly liberalism (no less than of non-scholarly liberalism) was to dispense with the christology of the NT.

Bultmannian Existentialism

Since liberalism was intimately associated with an optimism about the achievements of man and his gradually learning a correct way to live, the liberal bubble was punctured by World War I[21] which showed that man was somewhat more adept in learning a way to die. If liberalism gave us an image of the Jesus who taught man how to live and save himself, the tragic war created a need for a more traditional Christianity based on *God's* salvation of mankind in Jesus. The reaction against liberalism found eloquent spokesmen in Karl Barth in the area of systematic theology and Rudolf Bultmann in the area of biblical study. Because Bultmann is radical, many of his opponents tend to think of him as liberal; yet his NT theology is

---

peared in 1913; the English translation (Nashville: Abingdon), in 1970. The feasibility of bringing out an English edition of such an old book in a rather tight book market may reflect a revival of interest in liberalism (see note 16 above).

[21]When I place scholarly liberalism before World War I, I do not mean that there are not scholarly liberals in the field of christology today. (Fritz Buri and Schubert Ogden have written after Bultmann's heyday and have tried to reconcile his thought with liberal conclusions.) I mean simply that liberalism is no longer dominant in christological studies, especially among exegetes.

a categorical rejection of the liberalism of the pre-war period. Of course, he continues to accept the methodology developed by the liberal scholars in classifying stages of early Christian thought (as described above) and indeed has refined the methodology further, but he does not agree that the christology detected in these various stages and traced through them is a pure creation. I find it difficult to characterize exactly the relationship that Bultmann would establish between the christology of the NT writings and Jesus' evaluation of himself, but in some of his writing at least he is agnostic about the self-evaluation of Jesus.[22] Yet Bultmann would not think that the christology has distorted the import of Jesus as the liberals maintained. Rather there is a *functional equivalence* between the Church's christological proclamation and Jesus' proclamation of the kingdom of heaven.

It is in this functional equivalence that we see Bultmann's existential philosophy at work. Man has hope for escape from the vicious circle of futile existence only through a delivering action of God. Jesus came proclaiming that God was acting decisively in his own ministry and challenged man to accept this action of God. It is not clear to what extent Jesus uttered this challenge in terms of a christological self-evaluation, but the Church did give a christological evaluation when it demanded that men accept Jesus as Messiah and Lord. It is important to perceive that in such christological language the Church of the NT was equivalently offering the same challenge that Jesus offered. Thus, while the christology of the NT may not stand in demonstrable continuity with the christology of Jesus' ministry, the challenge offered by its christology stands in continuity with the challenge offered by Jesus' proclamation of the kingdom of heaven. Jesus preached the kingdom; the Church preached Jesus; functionally this preaching was equivalent. For that rea-

---

[22]Since Bultmann's writings are prolific and stretch over a span of nearly fifty years, it is not always easy to find an absolutely consistent stance. It is worth comparing *Jesus and the Word* (German original, 1926; paperback ed. New York: Scribners, 1958) and his article "The Primitive Christian Kerygma and the Historical Jesus" (German original, 1962; in *The Historical Jesus and the Kerygmatic Christ*, ed. C. E. Braaten and R. A. Harrisville; New York: Abingdon, 1964).

son it would be disastrous to dispense with the christology of the NT as the liberals had advocated—dispensing with christology would be tantamount to dispensing with the challenge that is the core of Christianity, a challenge that is primarily based on what God has done for man, rather than on what man can do for himself.

Moderate Conservatism

Bultmann's greatest influence was in the period from the 1920's to the 1950's.[23] Just as Bultmann's position was somewhat to the right and more conservative than that of the earlier scholarly liberals, I would judge that most christological scholarship today is somewhat to the right of Bultmann. (Thus, while the main body of NT scholarship has actually been moving to the right during the course of this century, any change in Catholic scholarship has involved a movement to the left, since for the first half of the century it remained in an isolated conservatism.) I would designate the majority position in contemporary christological scholarship as a moderate conservatism, even if some of the scholars I mention might be surprised to have themselves classified as conservatives. However, if I am right in diagnosing conservatism in christology as centered on the thesis that there is *a discernible continuity* between the evaluation of Jesus during the ministry and the evaluation of him in the NT writings, I find this thesis of continuity in most contemporary scholarly writing. Of course, this is no return to the extreme conservatism that I described as the first of my categories, for the contemporary moderates insist that there has been considerable development from Jesus to the NT writings, and they continue to employ with great precision the methodology of tracing the chronological growth of Christian thought first devised by the liberals. But they clearly posit a christology in the ministry of Jesus himself on which point Bultmann is not always definite.

I would see the main christological distinction among con-

---

[23]Bultmann's main works were translated into English decades after the German originals, and so his impact on English-speaking circles was somewhat delayed. John A. T. Robinson's discovery of the import of Bultmann in *Honest to God* (1963) is a good example.

temporary NT scholars as centered on the question of the kind
of christology detectable in the ministry of Jesus, *explicit or implicit christology*. Explicit christology is a christology evaluating
Jesus in terms of the titles known to the Jews from the OT or
intertestamental writings. It would be difficult to find serious
contemporary support for the thesis that Jesus used of himself
or accepted the "higher" titles of later NT christology, e.g.,
"Lord" in the full sense, "Son of God," or "God." (This does
not mean that scholars who deny Jesus' use of these titles are
saying that Jesus was not Lord, Son of God, or God; it may
mean that they regard the application of such designations to
have been the result of later Christian reflection on the mystery
of Jesus.) But there are serious exponents of explicit christology
who think that during the ministry Jesus referred to himself or
accepted designation as Messiah, or the Prophet, or the Servant
of God, or the Son of Man—the "lower" titles of christology.
This thesis of explicit christology was popular in the scholarship
of the 1950's and early 1960's and is still respectable today.
Among its adherents I could list O. Cullmann, C. H. Dodd, J.
Jeremias, V. Taylor and most of the Roman Catholic writers on
christology in the 1960's.[24]

However, in the last ten years, in Protestant and Catholic
writing alike, there is more acceptance of a thesis of *implicit
christology* wherein Jesus did not express his self-understanding
in terms of titles or accept titles attributed to him by others.
Rather he conveyed what he was by speaking with unique authority and acting with unique power. By his deeds and words
he proclaimed that the eschatological reign of God was making
itself present in such a way that a response to his ministry was a
response to God. Yet this implicit claim to uniqueness was not
phrased in titles reflecting the traditional expectations of Judaism. Among the scholars who tend toward implicit christology may be listed F. Hahn, R. H. Fuller, N. Perrin, some of
the post-Bultmannians in Germany, and Roman Catholic authors of the 1970's.[25]

---

[24]For a Catholic view see X. Léon-Dufour, *The Gospels and the Jesus of History* (Garden City: Doubleday, 1970 abridgment of a French original of 1963).

[25]See B. Vawter, *This Man Jesus* (Garden City: Doubleday, 1973). Also R. E.

Perhaps an example would help to illustrate the difference
between explicit and implicit christology and the respective implications. Respectable scholars, especially in England, still
maintain that Jesus referred to himself as the Son of Man, in
particular, as the Son of Man who would return as the judge of
the world. But a growing number of scholars reject such an explicit self-designation by Jesus.[26] If he spoke of the Son of Man,
he spoke of him as another figure yet to come.[27] But these
scholars would find an implicit christology in Jesus' statements
about the Son of Man. For instance, Luke 12:8-9 claims that
when the Son of Man comes, his judgment will be based on

Brown and P. J. Cahill, *Biblical Tendencies Today: An Introduction to the
Post-Bultmannians* (Washington: Corpus, 1969). A great deal of implicit christology is uncovered in modern studies of the parables and healings of Jesus.

[26]The "Son of Man" problem is much discussed today and I am giving above
only two approaches. Other scholars deny that there was a definite Son of Man
expectation in Judaism.

[27]All modern christology is based on the theory that the human knowledge of
Jesus was limited. In Catholicism this theory often runs against a popular misunderstanding which would claim that since Jesus was the Second Person of the
Blessed Trinity, he knew, even as man, all that God would know—a misunderstanding usually accompanied with the argument that the person is the subject
of knowledge and there was only one person in Jesus. Such an approach was un-
acceptable to the great scholastic theologians. Thomas Aquinas, *Summa Theo-
logica* III, q. 9, a. 1, ad 1, says: "If there had not been in the soul of Christ
some other knowledge besides his divine knowledge, he would not have known
anything. Divine knowledge cannot be an act of the human soul of Christ; it
belongs to another nature." Knowledge comes through the nature, and God and
man know in different ways: God's knowledge is immediate and non-concep-
tual; man's knowledge is through abstraction and is conceptual. Therefore divine knowledge is not simply transferable to a human mind. Precisely because
of their acknowledgment of this limitation, the scholastics posited special aids to
the human nature of Jesus so that he would know more than other men, e.g.,
Beatific Vision, infused knowledge. This is obviously a problem within the do-
main of systematic theology, and scholars like Rahner and Lonergan deny the
presence of such aids. Critical biblical scholars have been unable to detect their
presence; and most of us are willing to settle for the teaching of Chalcedon
(DBS 301, based on Heb 4:15) which made Jesus consubstantial with human
beings in all things except sin—and therefore consubstantial with us in limited
knowledge. (Hostile right-wing columnists have seized on this to alarm Catholics
with the news that scholars are now saying that Jesus was ignorant.) Of course,
a limitation of human knowledge does *not* mean that Jesus was not God; it
means he was man.

whether or not people have acknowledged or denied Jesus. Since in the long run final judgment must be based on whether or not men have acknowledged God, the centering of judgment around the acceptance of Jesus is a striking claim—ultimately a higher christology than that involved in whether or not Jesus thought of himself as the Son of Man.

I suspect that for the rest of the century scholarship will rock back and forth between explicit christology and implicit christology. (In my opinion the problem of Jesus' use or non-use of the Son of Man title is presently unresolvable, for there is simply not enough evidence about the contemporary Jewish use or understanding of this term.) But regardless of whether one detects explicit or implicit christology in the ministry of Jesus, the line of continuity to the Church's evaluation of him in the NT seems more firmly marked than was thought possible in scholarship earlier in the century. I would urge you who are College Teachers of Religion to stress this positive point to your students and, through them, to a wider lay and clerical audience in the Church. Above all, please make clear that when scholars are discussing the question of explicit and implicit christology, e.g., the question of whether or not Jesus ever referred to himself as the Messiah or accepted designation as Messiah,[28] those scholars who think that he did not use or accept this title are not necessarily detracting from the greatness of Jesus. Indeed, a greater claim can be made for Jesus if he did not find the title "Messiah" acceptable. It may mean that his conception of himself was so unique that the title did not match this uniqueness—the Church was able to call him Messiah successfully only when it reinterpreted the title to match Jesus' greatness. Thus, the ultimate tribute to what and who Jesus was may have been that every term or title in the theological language of his people had to be reshaped by his followers to do justice to him, including the title "God" itself.[29]

---

[28]Popular understanding of this problem is not helped by those (often polemicists) who tell people that scholars are now doubting whether Jesus knew he was the Messiah. The question is not whether Jesus knew he was the Messiah, for Jesus intuitively was aware who he was; the question is whether "Messiah," as that title was understood in his lifetime, satisfactorily described who he was.

[29]It is another false simplification that Catholic scholars are now doubting

My survey has stressed both a growth in scholarship in the twentieth century and a growth in christology in the first century. Obviously the first century and the NT were only the beginning of a longer quest to understand who Jesus is, a quest that stretched through Nicaea and which continues today. The Church has rejected some answers about Jesus and has embraced others as at least partially expressing her faith.[30] But as long as the Church exists, she must continue her struggle to find a still more adequate answer. The question posed by Jesus at Caesarea Philippi, "Who do men say that I am?", will never have an answer that exhausts the truth of his uniqueness until that day when he appears and "we shall see him as he is" (I John 3:2), no longer in a glass darkly, but "face to face" (I Cor 13:12).

---

whether Jesus knew he was God. Once more Jesus intuitively was aware who he was; the question is whether "God" as understood by a first-century Jew (namely, as the Father in heaven) could have described who Jesus was. Christians found "God" a satisfactory designation, but only after they had enlarged their understanding of the term to include the Son on earth. See R. E. Brown, *Jesus God and Man* (New York: Macmillan, 1967), 28-38, 95ff.

[30]Even the "true God of true God" of Nicaea does not end the search. The Roman Doctrinal Congregation (Holy Office) Declaration *Mysterium Ecclesiae* (1973) is most helpful in the struggle against a Catholic fundamentalism that does not realize the limited nature of dogmatic formulations. This Declaration acknowledges *limitations* imposed by the expressive power of language used at a particular time, by incomplete expressions of truth, by the fact that specific questions were being answered, and by traces left by the changeable conceptions of a given epoch. See the text in the Appendix.

PART TWO

CRISES IN ECUMENISM

The William Henry Hoover Lectures on Christian Unity

Introduction:
Modern New Testament Studies
and the Future of Ecumenism[31]

A Roman Catholic Viewpoint

When Dean Blakemore of the Disciples Divinity School invited me to give the Hoover Lectures—an honor that I doubly appreciate now that I have learned that I am the first Roman Catholic to speak in this distinguished series—he asked me to speak "within the broad range of Christian unity" and expressed the hope that I would make the issue biblical. I responded to the twofold subject with enthusiasm, for ecumenism and the Scriptures are topics intimately intertwined in my life and in the life of my Church.

First, *in my life,* in the sense that shortly after I began my teaching career in Bible at St. Mary's Seminary, Baltimore, I was asked to address the Faith and Order Conference of the World Council of Churches (Montreal, 1963), a group no Catholic had addressed before. And the address was to be part of a debate with Ernst Käsemann over pluralism in the NT and its impact on ecumenism. Later on, other ecumenical opportunities came my way, both from the Vatican Secretariat for Christian Unity and from the World Council of Churches. But, more im-

---

[31]The Hoover Lectures were given in Chicago on January 28-29, 1975, under the auspices of the Disciples Divinity House, with the cooperation of the Divinity School of the University of Chicago. Publication was stipulated by the invitation. Since I spoke from notes rather than from a text, the lectures are assuming here their complete form for the first time.

portant, my biblical interests have been oriented by problems raised at such ecumenical discussions. My book *Priest and Bishop*, which attempts to apply biblical criticism to the origins of the priesthood and the episcopate, came out of the Vatican-World Council discussion of apostolicity and out of the Lutheran-Catholic Dialogue in the U.S.A. on ministry. The latter Dialogue was also the point of origin for *Peter in the New Testament*.

Besides being woven together in my life, ecumenism and Scripture studies have gone together *in the life of my Church*. One could argue that the two most dramatic turnabouts in Catholicism in this century came in 1943 and in 1964. In 1943, after a third of the century in which Catholic officialdom had rigorously banned modern biblical criticism, Pope Pius XII issued the encyclical *Divino Afflante Spiritu* encouraging the use of criticism.[32] In 1964, after two thirds of a century in which Catholic officialdom ignored or rejected the ecumenical movement, the Vatican Council issued a decree on ecumenism that encouraged and even mandated Catholic participation. The Roman Catholic Church does not easily admit its mistakes, but those who can read between the lines of these documents will appreciate the immensity of the change involved. And the sequence of change was not accidental. The period from the 1940's to the 1960's was one of great progress for Catholic biblical scholars, free at last to follow the directions of critical investigation which brought them into increasing contact with their Protestant confreres. Consequently, when the ecumenical doors were thrown open, there was a core of Catholic biblical scholars who had the contacts and the background to enter into the dialogue—whence my own pilgrimage.

Those remarks explain the past and where we stand today, but I prefer in these lectures to turn to the future and to discuss problems that still divide Christians. Allow me to issue two cau-

---

[32]In the lecture which constitutes the first chapter of this book I have described at greater length the development of Catholic biblical criticism in the twentieth century. A more technical discussion can be found in *The Jerome Biblical Commentary*, ed. R. E. Brown *et al.* (Englewood Cliffs: Prentice Hall, 1968; London: Chapman, 1969), article 72, esp. ##3-9, 20-23.

tions so that you will not think that I am utterly without sense in speaking of the future of ecumenism. The first caution is that I am speaking in only one area and from only one aspect, the theological. I am aware that there are many non-theological areas where ecumenism has a future no matter how the problems I discuss here are resolved. Even if there is no resolution of Protestant and Catholic differences about the ordination of women, the papacy, and mariology (the topics I shall discuss in these lectures), the churches and Christians can and will work together for world justice, for peace, and for the alleviation of intolerance. These areas of ecumenical cooperation are more visible and, for many, more important than the theological topics I shall discuss. And even my theological topics have non-theological aspects that I shall not be able to treat. If the theological difficulties about the papacy were settled, financial considerations might prevent the union of the churches willing to accept a common spokesman. While theological consensus in the last few years has been a positive factor in ecumenical relations, this has been more than offset by the negative impact of declining church membership. If ecumenism seems to persuade Christians that it is no longer important to attend their own church, an ecclesiastical desire to survive will call into question the desirability of more ecumenism. If the ordination of women to the priesthood means that male clergy lose jobs, theological reasoning may well not be the deciding factor in this theological question. Therefore, when in these lectures I point out the theological direction that we might go, please do not conclude that I necessarily think it is the direction we shall go. I am only mapping out a road. I do not know whether we can get the money to build the road; whether access rights will be granted by those whose property or investment may be threatened by the road; whether motorists will like the road and want to travel it; and whether they will have the automobiles and gasoline to do so.

My second caution in speaking about the future of ecumenism involves my own limitations as a foreseer of the future. I join with Amos (7:14) in maintaining: "I am no prophet, nor a prophet's son"; but unlike Amos I am not going to deliver oracles. Yet I do not think that an uncertainty about our ability to foretell the future can spare us the sense that these are prophetic times. With the year 1975 we have entered the last quarter of the last century of the second millenium. Already we tend to speak of two thousand years of Christianity, but how much more shall we feel the mystique of time when finally we sign the date January 1, 2000—a future possibility for some of us! Millenarian enthusiasm will revive in many ways, some childish; but I do think that on January 1, 2000, a legitimate question of Christian self-examination can be asked. After two thousand years should not Christianity be able to present to the world a more unified witness to Christ than is now visible in our divisions and bitterness? It is more than embarrassing, it is frightening to reflect that Christianity was less divided on January 1, 1000 than it may be on January 1, 2000; for that first millenial anniversary antedated the formal split of East and West in 1054, as well as the Reformation and its aftermath. I say less divided that Christianity *may* be on January 1, 2000 precisely because I have great hope for this last quarter of the last century of the second millenium. We have come a long way in the past ten years in terms of Roman Catholic-Protestant relationship, and it is with the conviction that we can go a longer way in the next twenty-five years that I begin these lectures.

3.
The Meaning of Modern New Testament Studies for the Possibility of Ordaining Women to the Priesthood

I would like to begin by telling you of an experience I had which made me wonder whether I was looking into the future of this question. It happened last year in the main corridor of Union Theological Seminary where I teach. There were two people in the corridor. Walking toward me was a Jesuit seminarian from Woodstock College, dressed in secular clothing, brown suit, tie, etc. Walking ahead of me and thus passing him in the corridor was a Protestant woman seminarian wearing a black blouse, a clerical (Roman) collar—and, incidentally, a grey miniskirt. But this time at least it was the clerical collar that caught my attention. As the two passed one another, I wondered was I seeing a vignette of the future of two churches passing one another in the corridors of time.

The ordination of women to the priesthood is not yet a divisive factor in the relationship of the Roman Catholic Church and other churches. But it soon may become one as other churches with whom the Catholic Church is currently in dialogue adopt the practice; obviously I think of the Episcopal or Anglican Church. And it is difficult to believe that the problem will come to Catholicism only from outside relationships, for the question of ordaining women is so much a part of the trend of our times that it is certain to arise from within the

Catholic Church itself. The last quarter of this millenium is likely to be dominated by the continuing quest for the self-expression of the human person. Most issues that have had center stage in Catholic ethical reflection in recent years, birth control, divorce, and abortion, no matter how justified our opposition, still reflect a movement for people to determine their own destiny, not to have children if they do not want them, not to remain in hopeless marriages. On the American scene, in particular, there is now a determined movement for women to dictate their own destiny and not to have it dictated by men; and inevitably this has spilled over to the destiny of women within the Church. I would judge that inside Catholicism we have as much chance of avoiding a discussion of the ordination of women as we have had of avoiding a discussion of the other forms of self-determination I have mentioned—and perhaps as much chance of avoiding acrimony as well.

To begin, let me make it clear that I am speaking here about the ordination of women *to the priesthood*, not about a church ministry for women or even about women ministers. It is no accident that there has been much less dispute about the ordination of women in churches that call their clergy ministers[33] than has developed in churches that call their clergy priests. The ordination of women remains a divisive issue for the Church of Sweden, an area of Lutheranism that has retained the nomenclature of priests. We all know how divisive the issue has become in the Episcopal or Anglican Church. I predict that it will become an increasingly divisive issue in the Roman Catholic Church. Could it become a problem even for the Orthodox Churches if other churches whose eucharist they recognize ordain women? Now, why is there a difficulty about women priests, more than about women ministers? Is there something of the awe of entering divine mysteries captured in the concept of priesthood that is not captured in the concept of ministry? In any case, the sneering reference to a Christian priestess is a vis-

---

[33]Frequently in these churches the problem is not about ordaining women but about giving them respectable parish assignments. In other words the discrimination is on a more subtle level.

ceral reflection of a feeling that some find difficult to vocalize more precisely.

NON-THEOLOGICAL FACTORS

I shall discuss the question of ordaining women to the priesthood exclusively from a Roman Catholic perspective. Even though I know that the arguments pro and con frequently apply to other churches as well, I wish to remain in the ecclesiastical area I know best. In the Introduction to these lectures, I warned that I would treat problems only from a theological aspect, even though I knew that there were many non-theological factors that might determine the solution. The non-theological factors are so prominent in the question of ordaining women that I feel impelled to mention them briefly, lest my treatment sound utterly naive.

There is an *economic* factor, namely, job availability. This has been a particular obstacle to women in the ministry in Protestantism; for many of the large churches, Episcopal, Lutheran, Presbyterian, Methodist, United Church, have already more male clergy than they can place. But in Roman Catholicism there is a serious shortage of clergy. A prominent archbishop has predicted that by 1985 parishes in his diocese that have traditionally had three to five priests may have only one priest. Some bishops have begun to meet the clergy shortage by inviting nuns to serve virtually as curates in parishes, visiting the sick, distributing the eucharist, giving marriage counseling, etc. On a Carribean island where there are only two Catholic priests, on three Sundays out of four an individual Mass station will be tended by a sister who will read the Scriptures to the congregation, give a short homily, and distribute the eucharist. On the fourth Sunday a priest comes to say Mass. Such situations will eventually cause people to ask why, if sister does everything else,[34] she cannot consecrate the eucharist, so that they could have Mass every Sunday.

---

[34]The administration of the Sacrament of Penance (hearing confession) is a particular problem, for it requires a specialized knowledge of ethics and of

There are *social* factors involved in the ordination of women. Has the women's liberation movement really touched the lives of many women in Catholic parishes? Ours is a strong tradition of motherhood and family life. How would the sight of a woman in the pulpit, playing a leading role in the parish, affect the average Catholic wife, never mind the average Catholic husband? Some of the most vigorous critics of the new freedom of Catholic nuns, both as to dress and manner of life, have been Catholic married women. In other words, it is debatable whether it is better for the Catholic Church to lead the way by giving women pastoral leadership in parishes or to wait until there is a better climate for liberated women in ordinary Catholic life. The latter is obviously the more prudent choice; but whereas in so many other social questions the Church has been a follower, and even a reluctant follower, there are many who would like to see her lead in this question. "Lead" means, of course, that one can detect the way that things are likely to go.

If we wish to be honest, there are also *sexual* factors to be faced in ordaining women to the Catholic priesthood. Besides the usual threat to the male's identity that appears in any situation where women have authority over men, there is a special problem in Catholicism that no other church faces—a celibate parish clergy. Granted the Roman Church's clearly affirmed intention to retain a celibate clergy, if we consider ordaining women, are we to think of celibate women? If so, what about celibate men and celibate women working in close proximity in parish administration? Inevitably there will be instances where they fall in love, and so are we willing to pay the price of losses from the clergy and of scandal? (But then, without ordaining women, do we not already have losses and scandals?) More important, if we are to ordain women priests, we must have full-scale seminary training for women. I have mentioned that already in some dioceses nuns are being invited to serve in parish ministry in an unordained capacity, but often these sisters are given only a quick pastoral preparatory course of six months or less. This is better than nothing in an emergency situation, but it

canon law. However, since increasingly it is not a weekly ministration, it is a less pressing problem during a clergy shortage.

means that they will remain second-class citizens when compared to male clergy who have had a four-year seminary course. Moreover, the pastoral inadequacies that result from a patchwork training of these sisters will be used as proofs that women make inferior parish assistants. No, women in the priesthood means women in the seminaries. From my experience in a Protestant seminary that eagerly accepts women students, I would suspect that the presence of women would raise the intellectual tone of Catholic seminaries; but I know that many in the Church, not without reason, would regard it the height of imprudence to place in close proximity young women and young men destined for celibate lives. Others will reply that the problem of a celibate man coming to terms with half the human race is a problem which, if not faced in the seminary, will have to be faced after ordination, with even greater possibility of tragedy.

The thought of ordaining women as priests also raises *organizational* difficulties. If there are to be women priests, why not women bishops? And if women bishops, why not a woman . . . ? I shall allow you to fill in the blank; personally I am staggered at the thought of a woman monsignor. Madame, you may have come a long way, but after all!

There are even *international* factors involved in ordaining women to the Catholic priesthood. The push for women clergy is becoming familiar to American Catholics, but we are a church whose headquarters is in Italy and whose leadership is Italian. Can the ordination of women ever be a real possibility in the Catholic Church until the Italian women's liberation movement has had its day, a day which at the moment has scarcely dawned? I leave it up to those who have lived in Italy to say whether they can imagine a woman priest in an Italian parish. The same cultural difficulties might be faced by women priests in other Catholic countries, especially Third World countries. If the Roman Catholic Church is to act as a whole, the question may not be able to be settled on an Anglo-Saxon or American basis. Or is pluralism conceivable in a question like this?

And finally, not because I have mentioned all the factors but lest I go on forever, there are *ecumenical* factors to be dealt with in ordaining women to the priesthood. The most common

objection I have heard from Roman authorities against the ordination of women is that such an action would destroy the possibility of church union with the Orthodox. Episcopalian women
report that those who oppose the ordination of women in their
church frequently contend that such an action would destroy the
possibilities of union with Rome. (But what about the ecumenical obligations of the Episcopal or Anglican Communion to
Protestant churches that ordain women?) It is a valid principle
that a church should reflect very seriously whether a unilateral
action taken with regard to ministry will further divide Christians. But these are impatient times. Is it a serious possibility
that the possible implications for existing church divisions will
really stop women from seeking and obtaining ordination if
they can show that there is no divine prohibition against it? Ini-
tiative rather than caution launched the ecumenical movement;
it is dubious that caution can be successfully invoked on this
point above all.

A THEOLOGICAL FACTOR

With all these non-theological factors entering the consideration of women priests, you realize how partial is my contribution when I proceed to discuss a theological factor of the
question. Do not think me cowardly when I warn you that even
from a theological aspect *I am not going to give a firm answer
to whether or not women should be ordained as priests in the
Roman Catholic Church.* In part, this stems from my conception of the role of a theologian or a biblical scholar. I think that
we should be allowed to contribute significantly to the Church's
answer,[35] but I do not think that we can determine the answer
ourselves. Moreover, I am especially conscious of my own limitations in this particular question. I am no specialist in the roles
or abilities of women. I am unmarried. I grew up in a family
where my mother was the only woman. I do not know how

---

[35] In the lecture that constitutes the first chapter of this book I dedicated several pages to the role of the magisterium of the Church and its relation to
theologians.

women should dress in church, a knowledge that male ecclesiastics have claimed since Paul's day. And particularly embarrassing for a Catholic clergyman, I do not even know how nuns should dress. And so how should I be so reckless as to pass a judgment on whether or not there can be women priests? Indeed, I would think that until there are more Catholic women theologians, especially women willing to theologize within a framework of cooperation with the hierarchy (a two-way street, I recognize), we shall not have a Catholic theological quorum to do justice to the problem.

In attempting a contribution that is admittedly partial and inconclusive, I want to examine the impact of various Catholic ecclesiologies on the question. Despite the title of this lecture, "The Meaning of Modern New Testament Studies for the Ordination of Women," I do not plan to offer an exegesis of a number of NT texts, as I shall do in the subsequent lectures. This may displease some who think that the Christian answer to the problem of ordaining women lies in a text like I Cor 14:33-34: "As in all the churches of the saints, the women should keep silence in the churches,"[36] or perhaps farther back, in the creation story of Genesis. But here we enter the realm of hermeneutics. Since the Bible contains the word of God *in the words of men*, these texts reflect the sociology of God's people respectively in the first century A.D. and the eleventh century B.C. They cannot be repeated as normative today in a different sociology without first investigating whether the change of social condition does not require a different expression of God's will for His people. It is precisely this question of hermeneutics that I shall try to grapple with, faithful to my title "The *Meaning* of Modern New Testament Studies for the Ordination of Women," by showing how the acceptance or refusal of NT criticism shapes one's ecclesiology, and how one's ecclesiology or view of the Church is often decisive as to whether one thinks that women can or should be ordained.

---

[36] It has been suggested that this text is not genuinely Pauline but was added as a polemic against the Montanist movement where women prophets played an important role; if so, it would offset 11:5 which permits a woman to prophesy. The question needs more study.

There are many ecclesiologies or views of the Church flourishing in Catholicism today,[37] but for our purposes I shall distinguish three and apply their principles to the ordination question. Although I do not have the same affection for each of these three ecclesiologies, I shall endeavor to be descriptive, since in the long run it matters little which ecclesiology *I* approve or disapprove. What matters is how much influence each of these ecclesiologies has in Catholicism, for the ecclesiology that dominates may well tip the scales for or against ordaining women.

Blueprint Ecclesiology

The first ecclesiology is one that supposes that God has given us a blueprint of the Church in which all the basic structures and ways of sanctification were mapped out. For instance, God (or Jesus) specified the number of sacraments (seven in Catholic belief); He penciled in the structure in terms of deacon, priest, and bishop, including a supreme bishop. In the course of building the Church along the lines specified by the divine blueprint, succeeding generations may decide on different decorative schemes, remodel the facade, add conveniences, but not touch the main structure or the arrangement of the floors; for that is part of the edifice shaped by God on apostles and prophets with Christ as the capstone (Eph 2:20). By intrinsic logic, blueprint ecclesiology does not allow for the ordination of women, for they were not sketched by God into the hierarchical section of the building. Women are in the blueprint but chiefly as contributing tenants. We can distinguish two forms of blueprint ecclesiology, one based on the Bible, the other on Church Tradition.

"Bible blueprint ecclesiology" is usually based on the Gospels and Acts as evidence that God's intentions were vocalized by an omniscient Jesus who foresaw the future. He thought about the Church and clearly founded it during his ministry or immediately after the resurrection. He thought about sacra-

---

[37]Avery Dulles has caught this well from another angle in his book *Models of the Church* (New York: Doubleday, 1974) in which he considers the Church as institution, mystical communion, sacrament, herald, and servant.

ments and we have his instituting words for at least baptism and the eucharist. He structured the Church, for at the Last Supper he ordained the Twelve as its first priests; and they were to ordain others. He foresaw the Masses of the future by the instruction: "Do this in commemoration of me." In such a blueprint ecclesiology based on the Bible, it is clear that if Jesus wanted women priests, he would not have ordained only men. As one extremist Catholic writer has put it pithily: if Jesus wanted a woman priest, he would have ordained his mother. (I like to quote this to Protestant scholars who may be aware how unhistorical Protestant fundamentalism is but have never encountered its Catholic counterpart.)

Now, however, the biblical basis for such blueprint ecclesiology is shaken in Catholicism. In 1964 the Pontifical Biblical Commission issued an official Instruction[38] telling Roman Catholics that the Gospels are to be evaluated as developing first-century tradition, a tradition that begins with Jesus but goes beyond him through apostolic preachers to the evangelists —in other words, the basic ideas of *Formgeschichte* and *Redaktionsgeschichte*. The Instruction states clearly that the Gospels do not necessarily report the literal words of Jesus. With this introduction of history into the formation of the Gospels, almost every biblical presupposition of blueprint ecclesiology is brought into doubt. Did the historical Jesus think clearly of the Church when that term occurs in only one passage in the four Gospels ("You are Peter and upon this rock I shall build my Church," Matt 16:18), a passage which the majority of critical scholars regard as post-resurrectional.[39] Did the historical Jesus think about the structure of the Church? The evidence is that he spoke about the eschatological reformation of Israel, not about a different religion. Did the historical Jesus think about ordination?

[38]For the pertinent sections of this Instruction see the Appendix, noting the passages I have italicized. In the lecture that constitutes Chapter Two of this book I pointed out the impact of this Instruction for Catholic christology, and basically ecclesiology will be heavily influenced by christology.

[39]This text of Matthew will be discussed at greater length in the next lecture on Peter (Chapter Four). The Greek word for "church" occurs also in Matt 18:17, but there the reference is to the local assembly, not to the Church with a capital "C" as in Matt 16:18.

He chose the Twelve, but they were to sit on thrones judging the twelve tribes of Israel (Luke 22:30). There is no biblical evidence that he thought about any of his followers, male or female, as priests, since there were already priests in Israel.[40] The text "Do this in commemoration of me" is present in only one of the two eucharistic patterns that have come down to us, the Lucan-Pauline, not the Marcan-Matthean; and so some scholars regard it as a church reflection on Jesus' action. In any case, it needs to be balanced against another saying attributed to Jesus at the Last Supper which does not seem to envisage a continued series of eucharistic banquets: "I tell you that from now on I shall not drink of the fruit of the vine until the kingdom of God comes" (Luke 22:18). Above all and finally, the foundation of "Bible blueprint ecclesiology" is weakened by the fact that NT criticism makes it very unlikely that we can picture the historical Jesus as omniscient, foreseeing the future of the Church in detail.[41]

Yet it remains possible to date the blueprint later (the second century rather than the first) and to give the Holy Spirit rather than Jesus the role of the one who sketched it. We may call this "Tradition blueprint ecclesiology," for it is based on the Tradition of the post-NT church. Some basic ecclesiastical structure and sacraments, formerly attributed to the time of Jesus, were fixed by the time of Ignatius of Antioch (*ca.* 110) and the manner of ordination was regularized during the second century. The precise date is not important. What is important is that these developments in Tradition reflect a blueprint given to the Church by the Holy Spirit, so that no real change in them is possible *even when questions arise that were not posed in the second century*. The omniscient Third Person of the Trinity foresaw future needs and issues in drawing up the blueprint. (Notice that the approach in the blueprint outlook is one of forestalling future problems rather than of growth through en-

---

[40]Many of the scholars who doubt that the historical Jesus thought in terms of the Church, sacraments, ordination, priests, etc., do not question the validity of such features in Christianity. As we shall see, these features can be looked upon as *later* developments in God's plan for His people.

[41]See footnote 27 above.

countering them, precisely because divine omniscience is seen to be at stake.) Later innovations in such a vital issue as ministry, e.g., the ordination of women, would imply that the Spirit had allowed the Church to be in error for almost two millenia. The point of challenge to this ecclesiology is the irreformability of the Tradition in matters that were not in question at the time the Tradition was shaped. And once again an official document of the Roman Catholic Church has created doubts about blueprint ecclesiology by calling attention to the historical conditioning of dogma and the consequent necessity of taking into account the questions that shaped the original Tradition. I refer to *Mysterium Ecclesiae* issued by the Doctrinal Congregation (Holy Office) in 1973, partially as a response to Hans Küng.[42] While this statement defends the concept of infallibility, it cautions Catholics that dogmatic positions can be phrased in terms that reflect "the changeable conceptions of a given epoch" and are usually taken in light of specific questions. Certain formulations may have to give way to new expressions, and truths at first expressed incompletely may only later receive a fuller expression. If such change of conception and expression is possible, how then can one be sure that the practice of ordaining only males that has existed for 1900 years may not represent a changeable and incomplete understanding of priestly ministry which needs a newer and fuller expression in light of a question being asked today but which was not asked in the second century?

Blueprint ecclesiology, whether based on Bible or on Tradition, is not dead; but it has little scholarly popularity. More important for Roman Catholics, its chief presuppositions can be questioned on the basis of official Roman Church documents. Let us look then at other ecclesiologies and their implications for the ordination of women.

Erector-Set Ecclesiology

At the opposite pole from blueprint ecclesiology is the thesis that Christians are free to go ahead and build the Church as utility directs. God (or Jesus) gave a commission to build a

---

[42]See the Appendix for the excerpt pertinent to this discussion.

community, but no blueprint. He gave some of the components, like pieces in an erector set, but no book of instructions, other than that the Church should be so built as to serve well the people of God who live in it. The scientific historical consciousness that has called into doubt the presuppositions of blueprint ecclesiology has served as a catalyst in moving Catholics to the opposite extreme.[43] If Jesus did not specify everything, and if many ecclesiastical developments were the product of the Holy Spirit's leading the Christian community, why cannot the Holy Spirit lead in another direction at a later period? Let me give an example. From the NT it appears that the clear conceptualization of the Christian priesthood came only after the destruction of the Jerusalem Temple in A.D. 70.[44] When the Jewish levitical priesthood no longer offered sacrifice in the Temple, Christians came to see more clearly that their eucharistic meal was *the* Christian sacrifice and that those who presided at it could be called priests. It is at the end of the first century that we find in this connection an appeal by Christians to the prophecy of Mal 1:11: "For from the rising of the sun unto its setting my name is great among the nations; and everywhere they bring sacrifice to my name and a pure offering." But the question of who would serve as priests was still in flux as we see from the *Didache* (turn of the century?) where, while prophets were permitted to celebrate the eucharist, the role of a more regular clergy was encouraged. Eventually the practice of a public ordination by a bishop was seen to fit best the needs of the Church. Now, in such a reconstruction of the origins of priestly designation, obviously history and sociology entered in: the way the Church structured its ministry was affected by its life-situation. If this is

---

[43]In the lecture that constitutes Chapter Two of this book, I pointed out that the same shift from one extreme to another has been true in Catholic christologies. See footnote 16. Perhaps I should be careful, however, in describing my picture of erector-set ecclesiology as an extreme. In order not to create a straw man I have allowed the Holy Spirit a place in this ecclesiology. There may be Roman Catholics who would reduce Church development entirely to sociological and historical causes without seeing the intervention of God in the Person of the Holy Spirit. That would be even more extreme.

[44]For the exegetical basis for the remarks that follow, see my *Priest and Bishop* (New York: Paulist, 1970; London: Chapman, 1971).

so, why cannot the history and sociology of *our* time guide the Church to a different procedure and a different set of candidates? If Church needs can be better met by the ordination of women, why not introduce the practice?

To many this may sound like the ecclesiology of the Reformation (and of the left wing of the Reformation at that) rather than an ecclesiology that could have followers in Roman Catholicism. But I would venture that such a concept of the Church has many adherents today, not only among young Catholics but even among older clergy, religious, and laity reacting against the theology which they were taught and which they now find historically questionable. In place of a historically dubious blueprint ecclesiology they tend to construct a sociological model of the Church that may be equally insensitive to the complexities of history. It is no accident that in more radical Catholicism today there is a pronounced tendency to resist the designation of the clergy as priests, preferring to substitute the term "minister." As I have pointed out, the ordination of women has caused less difficulty in many Christian churches that refer to their clergy as ministers; it would probably cause little difficulty in a Catholic community that no longer thinks of its clergy as priests.

In-Between Ecclesiology

I have no convenient designation for an ecclesiology intermediate between the blueprint and erector-set ecclesiologies. This is an ecclesiology where the pieces for building are provided as in an erector set but where God has not left the builders without a booklet of instructions—thus neither a blueprint nor an invitation to build anything you want. As in erector-set ecclesiology the criterion of the serviceability of the house is invoked, but so is the criterion of the will of Christ and the determinative guidance of the Spirit.

What can the will of Christ for the Church mean if one is not talking about a detailed blueprint left by Jesus?[45] Open to

---

[45]Notice the tendency to talk about the will of *Christ* as distinct from a blueprint left by *Jesus*. Most biblical scholars would recognize that it was only after the resurrection that Jesus' followers came to understand him as the Mes-

the results of biblical criticism, the upholders of "in-between ecclesiology" recognize the serious possibility that Jesus the Jew thought in terms of the reform of Israel and not specifically in terms of a separate Church with ordination and sacraments. But they recognize other historical facts that served to give direction to the community he left behind. For instance, the historical Jesus chose the Twelve who eventually came to function as apostles, and so the renewed Israel was not without leadership. Paul, converted by a vision of the risen Jesus, thinks of a hierarchy of charisms in the community, and apostleship is listed first. If there is no certainty that the sacraments of baptism and the eucharist can be linked to institutional words of the historical Jesus, nevertheless Christian baptism has a historical connection with the baptism that Jesus underwent at the hands of John, and the eucharist has a basis not only in the Last Supper but also, and perhaps primarily, in the meals at which the risen Jesus appeared to his disciples. History and sociology almost certainly played a role in the development of Church structure, especially the pattern of the single bishop and the college of presbyters which had emerged by the end of the first century; but our earliest testimonies to this structure see it as symbolically preserving the model of Jesus surrounded by his disciples. And so the will of Christ has meaning in this ecclesiology, even if the working out of that will is conceived in a subtler way than is proposed in blueprint ecclesiology.

Yet precisely because there is no blueprint, it is not inconceivable in this ecclesiology that in later ages in the face of new historical circumstances the Church can continue in its discovery of Christ's will—a discovery that may imply change. (But notice that it is a question of discovering Christ's will and not simply of finding the best sociological response.) What can

---

siah or the Christ in the sense in which Christians now use that term (a suffering Messiah who does not establish a political empire)—Mark 8:27-33 has Peter acclaim Jesus as the Messiah during the ministry but in an inadequate way that Jesus corrects. Therefore, in speaking of the will of *Christ* ecclesiologists are going beyond the ministry to the risen Lord who acts through the Spirit. Classical church statements attribute the institution of sacraments and church order to Jesus Christ the Lord and not simply to what a modern scholar would call the Jesus of the ministry.

change and what cannot change? There is no hard and fast rule. A sense of apostolicity means that some past decisions made within the Church under the guidance of the Spirit of Christ are thought to be normative for the future, just so that the future will remain in continuity with the past. A sense that Christ's will is not yet fully discovered means that other past decisions can cede to new decisions made under the guidance of the Holy Spirit.

The strength of "in-between ecclesiology" is that it combines the better elements of the two other ecclesiologies, "blueprint" and "erector-set." Its weakness is the lack of predictable answers. The practitioners of blueprint ecclesiology will, as I have said, surely oppose the ordination of women to the priesthood. The practitioners of erector-set ecclesiology will just as surely support it. But one cannot predict how the practitioners of in-between ecclesiology will respond. On the one hand, the age-long custom of ordaining only men will not be easily dismissed by them as the vestige of a primitive sociology. On the other hand, they may judge that the breaking down of human barriers by the grace of Christ, the barriers of origin, race, and social rank, will only be complete when the barrier of sex is broken within the Church. They may see equality of women in ministry as the final working out of Gal 3:28: "There is neither Jew nor Greek; there is neither slave nor free; there is neither male nor female; for you are all one in Christ Jesus."

Let me illustrate the way practitioners of in-between ecclesiology may disagree regarding the application of one theological principle to the question of women priests. In Roman Catholic theological symbolism the priest is called "another Christ." Every Christian should be another Christ, but the priest is thought to represent Christ in a special way as one through whom God communicates grace, especially sacramental grace, to His people. Now, in Christ the Word became flesh as a male, and some will argue that the priestly role as another Christ is more easily personified by a male. Others will choose to attach the symbolism not to maleness but to humanity. For them the wonder of the Christian mystery is that God's grace came to us through a fellow man, i.e., through a human being like us in everything except sin. Because of biological necessity the human being could be of only one sex, but it has never been the thrust of christology to put primary stress on the fact that the sex was male rather than female. If the theology of the priest as another Christ is meant to draw attention to the continued mediatorship of *humanity* in God's giving of grace, one might argue that a priesthood involving both males and females is a better symbol of humanity and overcomes the biological limitation of the incarnation. In short, there can be honest and intelligent disagreement among theologians adhering to an in-between ecclesiology on how to apply an accepted maxim to the question of ordaining women.

* * *

I have now finished discussing these three ecclesiologies that I see embraced by different Catholics and explaining how each would respond to the possibility of women priests. I warned that I was not going to attempt any personal solution,[46] and frankly I have no idea which ecclesiology will win out or dominate. "Blueprint ecclesiology" is clear-cut and firm and will attract those who dislike ambiguities—this probably includes most traditional parishioners, as well as church authorities. "Erector-set ecclesiology" appeals to the heart and will attract the enthusiastic and the free who with vibrancy and vitality are sure that the future is theirs—it will scarcely appeal to those already in authority. "In-between ecclesiology" will be embraced by Catholics of a reflective nature who put emphasis on the "middle-way" and on balance, but what may appear to

---

[46]Pedagogically, it seems obvious to me that no matter what the ultimate decision in the Roman Catholic Church about the ordination of women as priests, a better context for that decision will be created by giving women public roles in relation to the celebration of the eucharist, e.g., allowing younger girls to serve at the altar, having women lectors, incorporating women into dialogue sermons, and having women distribute the eucharist. Outside the sphere of eucharistic celebration, an extraordinarily important step is the encouragement of women theologians, the constitution of theology schools for Catholic women, and the introduction of women professors into Catholic seminaries. When all of these things are done, we may be in a much better position to discuss intelligently the ordination of women as priests.

them as a balance between firmness and freedom may appear to others as fickleness. And those who preach balance rarely change the world.

And so there we have it: the firm, the free, and the fickle. Which of the three has the answer? If I am wary of predicting the future, it is because I remember that no one in the Catholic Church in 1955, not Pope or bishop or theologian, could have predicted what the Catholic attitude toward ecumenism would be in 1965. Am I wrong in 1975 in suspecting that the Holy Spirit who moved the Roman Catholic Church through an amazing decade of change with regard to ecumenism might very well move the Church through another amazing decade of change as regards the role of women?

In the Gospel of John as a sequel to the story set at the well in Samaria, when the disciples returned from their shopping spree, they were shocked to find Jesus in conversation with a woman. But, John (4:27) tells us, not one of them dared to ask him "What do you want?" That curious failure to ask Jesus what he wanted of a woman has endured in the Church all too long. In this lecture I have not expressed much personal opinion, but there is one thing I am sure of. In the last quarter of the last century of the second millenium the disciples of Jesus must finally ask the question—the Church must come before its Master and ask point blank: "In these times and in these circumstances when we worship God in Spirit and truth (John 4:24), what is it that *you* want of a woman?"

(*Appended Note:* This lecture was given in January 1975. On April 18, 1975 Pope Paul VI, in addressing a committee studying the Church's response to the International Women's Year, spoke these words: "If women did not receive the call to the apostolate of the Twelve and therefore to the ordained ministry, they are however invited to follow Christ as disciples and collaborators." Some newspapers interpreted this as a definite statement that the Church can never ordain women. Yet in 1975 it was publicly announced in Rome that the Papal Theological Commission and the Pontifical Biblical Commission would study the role of women in the ministry including the question of ordination. The Biblical Commission only began its discussions of the question on April 8th, and so it is difficult to see that the Pope's remarks were meant to block further scholarly discussion of the question. Within a week of the papal address the Archbishop of Canterbury announced that he saw no theological obstacle to the ordination of women. That the Roman Catholic and Anglican Communions cannot simply ignore one another's position on this matter was dramatized when in that same month of April the first Episcopal eucharistic service was permitted within the walls of the Vatican.)

4.
The Meaning of Modern New Testament Studies for an Ecumenical Understanding of Peter and a Theology of the Papacy

The subject of my previous lecture, the ordination of women to the priesthood, is only now becoming an obstacle to Christian unity. Here I turn to a divisive issue of long-standing within Christianity; perhaps, indeed, the most divisive issue: the role and claims of the Pope. Membership in the National Dialogue between Lutherans and Roman Catholics has shaped my treatment of this issue as reflected in the twofold thrust of my title: "An Ecumenical Understanding of *Peter* and a Theology of the *Papacy*." Three years of discussion within the Dialogue itself showed me how future developments in attitudes toward the Papacy might be healing.[47] But what may have been more influential was my participation in a committee spun off from the Dialogue. Realizing the wide area that would have to be covered in discussing this subject, the leaders of the Dialogue commissioned a separate biblical investigation of the role of Peter. John Reumann, a Lutheran scholar, and I were delegated to gather a team of scholars to do this ecumenical study which

---

[47]The results of the Dialogue have been published as *Papal Primacy and the Universal Church* (Lutherans and Catholics in Dialogue V; Minneapolis: Augsburg, 1974).

lasted two years. And it is from the results of that NT investigation[48] that I speak here of Peter as well as of the Papacy.

How can Catholics and Protestants come to a meeting of
minds on the Papacy or on Peter's role? Especially how can
there be agreement with Lutherans whose historical relations to
the Papacy were bitter to the point that sometimes the Pope
was identified as the antichrist? Even if we leave aside emotion,
the immensity of the intellectual problem becomes apparent
from the following three statements of the First Vatican Council on Peter and the Papacy:[49]

> If anyone says that the blessed Apostle *Peter* was not con-
> stituted by Christ the Lord as the Prince of all the Apostles
> and the *visible head of the whole Church militant,* or that
> he received immediately and directly from Jesus Christ our
> Lord only a primacy of honor and not *a primacy of true
> and proper jurisdiction,* let him be anathema.

> If anyone says that it is not according to *the institution of
> Christ* our Lord himself, that is, by divine law, *that St.
> Peter has perpetual successors* in the primacy over the
> whole Church; or if anyone says that *the Roman Pontiff* is
> not the successor of St. Peter in the same primacy, let him
> be anathema.

> If anyone says that the Roman Pontiff has only the office
> of inspection or direction, but not *the full and supreme
> power of jurisdiction* over the whole Church, not only in
> matters that pertain to faith and morals, but also in mat-
> ters that pertain to the discipline and government of the
> Church throughout the whole world; or if anyone says that
> he has only a more important part and not *the complete
> fullness of this supreme power;* or if anyone says that this
> power is not *ordinary and immediate* over each and every

---

[48]Published as *Peter in the New Testament,* ed. R. E. Brown *et al.* (New
York: Paulist, 1973 and London: Chapman, 1974).

[49]Slightly corrected translation from *The Church Teaches* (St. Louis: Herder,
1955). The Latin original may be found in the *Enchiridion Symbolorum,* ed. H.
Denzinger and A. Schönmetzer (23rd ed.; Freiburg: Herder, 1963) ##3055,
3058, 3064. The grammar of anathematized negative statements is awkward for
the uninitiated, and so I have used italics to make apparent the main points
being affirmed.

church or over each and every shepherd and faithful member, let him be anathema.

Modern scholars, both biblical exegetes and theologians, would want clarification of these statements of Vatican I. A biblical exegete would want to ask at least these two questions. First, how is the role of the Bishop of Rome (Roman Pontiff) who claims succession to Peter related to the role(s) of Peter actually described in the NT? Second, how genuinely historical are the role(s) of Peter described in the NT? These questions would be important because there is an element of apparent historical affirmation in the first two statements quoted above: the Pope is given the same primacy as Peter, and Peter's primacy is described as a primacy of true and proper jurisdiction. The theologian would want to ask at least this question about the third declaration of Vatican I: How does full, supreme, ordinary and immediate jurisdiction over every church and over every faithful member leave any freedom in the Church, any ability to reform the Church against possible abuses in the Papacy?

In the ecumenical dialogue, knowing that there are such biblical and theological questions, does the Catholic scholar simply repeat the statements of Vatican I so that no progress is possible? And if he does not, how does he remain loyal to his Church's teaching? Fortunately now (and that is what makes the present such a wonderful time for dialogue) there are shifts within official Roman Catholic attitudes that make a middle road possible, one of loyalty and progress at the same time. In 1964 the Roman Pontifical Biblical Commission issued an *Instruction on the Historical Truth of the Gospels*[50] which officially teaches that the Gospels are not literal, chronological accounts of the words and deeds of Jesus, even though based on memories and traditions of such words and deeds. Apostolic preaching has reshaped those memories, as has also the individual viewpoint of each evangelist who selected, synthesized, and explicated the apostolic traditions that came down to him. As we shall see, such a modifying reassessment of the historicity of the Gospels casts light on how the statements of Vatican I bear-

---

[50]See the Appendix for the pertinent excerpt from this Instruction.

ing on the historical role of Peter may need to be reinterpreted by the introduction of distinctions that were not conceivable for a previous generation of Catholic scholars.

But, you may well ask, is it legitimate for a Catholic now to reinterpret statements made a hundred years ago by participants at a Council who were not familiar with the biblical and historical methods we employ today? Here we are helped by a second official document of the Roman Catholic Church, which is also useful in meeting the theological objection that I mentioned above. I refer to *Mysterium Ecclesiae*,[51] the 1973 declaration of the Doctrinal Congregation (former Holy Office) implicitly aimed at Hans Küng. This document goes farther than the Catholic Church has ever gone before in recognizing the historical conditioning of the formulations of Church dogma. The Roman Catholic Church, which in the 1960's came to grips with the historical conditioning of the Gospels, has now begun to come to grips with the historical conditioning of subsequent Tradition. In particular, *Mysterium Ecclesiae* says that in considering past pronouncements of Catholic doctrine we must take into account: (a) the expressive power of the language used at a certain point in time and particular circumstances; (b) the fact that sometimes a dogmatic truth is expressed only incompletely, needing at a later date and in a broader context of faith and knowledge a fuller and more perfect expression; (c) that a pronouncement may have been meant to solve only certain questions and that this limited scope must be taken into account in interpreting the pronouncement; (d) that sometimes the formulas are expressed in the changeable conceptions of a given epoch and may need new expressions which present more clearly or completely the genuine meaning. If a Catholic scholar takes seriously these four important qualifications, he is certain-

---

[51]See the Appendix for the pertinent excerpt. In the previous lecture (Chapter Three) on the possibility of ordaining women, I cited these same two documents as weakening a blueprint ecclesiology, based on the Bible or on Tradition. In this series of lectures which concerns the future of ecumenism I have deliberately chosen to bring forward church documents, precisely to underline that the possibilities of progress are not dependent merely on the dreams of liberal theologians.

ly not disloyal if he points out that the statements of Vatican I have biblical and historical limitations and that Vatican II offers the possibility of a more complete formulation of a theology of the Papacy.

That, in fact, the statements of Vatican I were not an insurmountable obstacle to ecumenical progress has been shown by the Roman Catholic—Lutheran discussions of Peter and the Papacy. Biblical and theological scholars from the two traditions were able to produce studies which considerably moved forward the discussion.[52] Let me share with you my analysis of the key points of the progress. (I shall refer throughout to "our" discussions, since, as I have explained, I was part of the respective committee and dialogue group; but obviously the analysis is my own and I take responsibility for it.)

THE ROLES OF PETER IN THE NEW TESTAMENT

Three factors were of significant help in our approach to Peter's position in NT thought. The *first* was a firm resistance to anachronism. Much of the past consideration of the NT evidence was influenced by Catholic—Protestant arguments about the relation of the Pope to Peter. We stated firmly that the Papacy in its developed form cannot be read back into the NT and that it would help neither papal opponents nor papal supporters to have the model of the Papacy before their eyes when discussing the role(s) of Peter. A consideration of the NT should avoid the imposition of "loaded" terms such as primacy and jurisdiction. The *second* helpful factor was that for the most part we considered the NT evidence in the historical order, fol-

---

[52]It was interesting to see the reactions of the extreme right-wing of the Catholic press (discussed in Chapter One above) to the statement of the Lutheran-Catholic Dialogue on the Papacy. Even though the Dialogue was sponsored by the Bishops' Committee for Ecumenical Affairs, the statement was written off as virtually heretical because of differences from the statements of Vatican I. The factor of the historical conditioning of the latter statements to which the Dialogue drew careful attention was completely ignored, and the same fundamentalist stance that this press has shown with regard to Scripture was reaffirmed in regard to doctrinal statements.

lowing the sequence of composition: the Pauline Letters, Acts,[53] Mark, Matthew, Luke, John, and the Petrine Epistles. Past discussions have often begun with or been dominated by Matt 16:16-19, the "You are Peter" passage. For instance, almost half of Oscar Cullmann's *Peter: Disciple, Apostle, Martyr,* a real breakthrough in Protestant interest in Peter, is devoted to the Matthean text. And this was a natural attitude in Catholic scholarship as well when Matthew was thought to be the first Gospel written by an eyewitness of Jesus' ministry,[54] for then one might assume that any Christian in NT times who knew the Jesus tradition would have known that Jesus had designated Peter as the rock on which the Church would be built. But if Matthew is seen as a relatively late Gospel and the sole witness for this saying of Jesus, then one must face the possibility that Paul withstood Peter at Antioch knowing him as the Rock (since he calls him Cephas) but not knowing the explanation of that name given by Matthew. The Matthean text, however early its origins, makes its written appearance in the last third of the century precisely when other NT writings were using foundational language for apostles. The post-Pauline Epistle to the Ephesians (2:19-20) speaks of "the household of God, built upon the foundation of apostles and prophets";[55] and Rev 21:14 reports that the twelve foundations of the wall of the heavenly Jerusalem had on them the names of the twelve apostles of the Lamb.[56] The *third* helpful factor was the progress of NT schol-

---

[53]The consideration of Acts after the Pauline Letters instead of after Luke is the one exception made to historical sequence. We offered this explanation: "Our sequence does not imply in any way that Acts has a historical value equal to that of Paul's letters when they are both describing the same events. Our sequence in this instance is topical, i.e., it is based on the fact that Paul and Acts describe the same or roughly contemporary events pertaining to Peter." For chronology, see footnote 8 above.

[54]This was a position imposed under the requirement of internal assent by the Roman Biblical Commission at the beginning of the century. For the freedom now granted Catholics with regard to such decrees see Chapter One and the Appendix.

[55]The "apostles" in the Ephesians text are not to be taken in the Lucan sense of the Twelve but in the Pauline sense which is wider ranging. See my *Priest and Bishop* (footnote 44 above), 48-63.

[56]Interestingly, Revelation (Apocalypse) seems to preserve two strains. The

arship beyond a fascination with the purely historical. In times past the discussion often centered on the *ipsissima verba* of Jesus with regard to Peter or on the precise position attributed to Peter by Paul in Galatians. Because of the chronological sequence in which we placed the NT works, we noted that the image of Peter was more prominent in the NT works written after his death than in those written during or immediately after his lifetime (Pauline Letters, Mark). Thus, a discussion of the NT must take into account the growing image of Peter in the mind of many late-first-century Christians and not simply the role or roles of Peter during his lifetime.

I want now to go through almost kaleidoscopically some insights that came to me from our study of the various Peter passages in the NT. Let me begin with well-known dispute between Paul and Cephas in Antioch (Gal 2:11ff.). While Paul is somewhat sharp with this "so-called pillar" (2:9) of the Jerusalem church, what struck me was the extent to which Paul mentioned Cephas to a predominantly Gentile community which he had evangelized himself. Cephas is mentioned without preliminary introduction, so we must assume that the Galatians knew about him. Evidently, even when the Gospel was preached by a non-eyewitness of the ministry of Jesus, such as Paul, Peter was part of the story of Jesus communicated to believers. The existence of a Cephas-party at Corinth (I Cor 1:12) is another testimony that in the 50's Peter was the best-known of the Twelve.

The study of Peter's role in the Book of Acts has often centered on whether Peter or James had the dominance in the mother-church of Jerusalem, but the fascination with that question may well stem from a presupposition that the primary problem is who was the first Pope and was there a succession to a primitive Papacy. From our discussions another solution seemed to me to emerge: not Peter over James or vice versa, nor Peter followed by James, but two men having very different functions at Jerusalem. Peter was the first of the Twelve who

---

Twelve as such were not part of Church structure; their role was eschatological (Luke 22:30); and so they are appropriately placed in a Jerusalem that descends from heaven. Yet some or all the Twelve doubled as missionary apostles, and so the foundational image that was characteristic of apostles was used of them.

were to sit on thrones judging the tribes of the renewed Israel, a once-for-all eschatological company who were not part of Church structure[57] and who remained at Jerusalem in the early days because that was to be the place of final judgment. When the community grew and administrative structure was necessary, the Twelve refused to be involved in administration and insisted that others be appointed (Acts 6:3-4). The administrative structure that emerged for the Jerusalem church involved James and the elders; and because of Jerusalem's centrality for Jewish Christians, James exercised an authority over churches in Palestine and Syria.[58] Thus James had an episcopal or even archiepiscopal role at Jerusalem even if he is never called a bishop in the NT, whereas, to the best of our knowledge, Peter never served as the bishop or local administrator of any church, Antioch and Rome included.[59]

Treating Mark as the first of the written Gospels, we noted on the one hand that therein Peter is clearly the most important or prominent of the Twelve, and on the other hand Mark is the least sparing of the Gospels in stressing the imperfections of Peter. Peter's messianic confession of Jesus is clearly treated as inadequate, so that the description of Peter as a Satan who thinks the thoughts of men rather than of God is particularly

---

[57]See footnote 56 above. I would see the story of Ananias and Sapphira (Acts 5:1-11) as illustrative of the earliest conception of Peter's function as chief of the Twelve: there he serves as a divinely empowered judge striking dead those who defile the purity of the renewed Israel. The judging power was institutionalized eventually as the power to bind and loose.

[58]The letter sent out from Jerusalem to be applied to those dwelling in Antioch, Syria, and Cilicia regulating the relationship of Gentile and Jewish Christians in those areas (Acts 15:23ff.) incorporates the position taken by James in the Jerusalem discussions.

[59] See my *Priest and Bishop* (footnote 44 above), 53-54. Later Church writers were anachronistic in calling Peter a bishop of Rome. In their time the supreme authority in the Church resided in bishops, and they expressed their appreciation of Peter's authority in the early Church by speaking of him as the bishop of Antioch or of Rome. The statement that he was not a bishop does not in any way take away from the authority that he possessed as the first among the Twelve. The distinction between Peter's real authority and the anachronistic language used in later periods to describe that authority—in other words, the problem of the inadequacy of theological language—is very important in discussing the statements about Peter in Vatican I.

harsh (Mark 8:27-33). Yet there was no strong tendency in our group to accept the hypothesis advanced with different nuances by scholars such as J. Schreiber, T. J. Weeden, and W. H. Kelber that Mark described the Twelve in a hostile way almost as if they had become the spokesmen of a false christology or false eschatology.[60] The very extravagance of this hypothesis was a reminder that the one Gospel written close to Peter's lifetime (late 60's?) made no attempt to glorify him or to smooth over his inadequacies.

The picture in Luke is quite different. As part of his general tendency to polish the image of the Twelve, Luke either omits or modifies some of the Marcan scenes most unfavorable to Peter. For instance, Peter's failure to appreciate the place of suffering in the messiahship of Jesus is excised, as is Jesus' rebuke, "Get behind me, Satan." The denials of Jesus by Peter are softened because at the Last Supper Peter is included in the praise of those who have continued with Jesus in his trials (22:28). Indeed, Peter is singled out for a special role: "I have prayed for you that your faith may not fail. And when you have turned again, strengthen your brothers" (22:32). Thus Luke sets

---

[60]In my opinion one can refute this hypothesis on purely exegetical grounds. But in this ecumenical lecture I do not want to gloss over possible differences between Protestants and Catholics, and so I should report that many Catholics (including myself) would have trouble with this hypothesis on theological grounds, namely, that it is inconsistent with the inerrancy of the Scriptures. Catholics have no simplistic or fundamentalistic principle of inerrancy. Leaving aside historical and scientific statements in the Bible, Catholics are not bound to believe even that all religious statements or teachings in the Bible are inerrant. (We note Job 14:13-22 where the author specifically raises the thesis of an afterlife and then categorically denies its possibility.) But Vatican II did bind Catholics to hold the inerrancy of what is taught in the Scriptures *for the sake of our salvation* (see Appendix). Since the Roman Catholic Church and many other Christian Churches adhere firmly to the apostolicity of the Church, how can one reconcile such inerrancy with the thesis that one of Mark's principal intentions in writing his Gospel was to have the Christians of his church believe that the Twelve were the chief spokesmen of a false christology or a false eschatology? Such a thesis is quite different from the suggestion that Mark retained the tradition that the followers of Jesus, including the Twelve, understood Jesus inadequately during his ministry and had to be rebuked by him, so that it was only after the resurrection that the Twelve became proclaimers of Christian faith.

up a continuity between the frailer Peter of the ministry of Jesus and Peter the strengthener who becomes the chief apostolic spokesman at Jerusalem in the Book of Acts. As a factor in this continuity Luke (alone among the Gospels) preserves the tradition that among the Twelve it was to Peter that Jesus first appeared (24:34). Thus, in a Gospel written in or near the 80's, Peter had clearly emerged as the most important church figure among those who followed Jesus during his ministry.

In this treatment of Peter, Luke is harmonious with Matthew. I have reported that we did not concentrate on Matt 16:17-19 in any isolated way, but we did come to a significant agreement that much of what is peculiar to Matthew in that Caesarea Philippi scene is probably post-resurrectional in origin. You will remember that at Caesarea Philippi Mark has Peter confess Jesus as the Messiah, a confession to which Jesus responds by ordering him to silence (Mark 8:29-30). Luke 9:20-21 agrees substantially with Mark; but Matt 16:16-19 has both a longer confession by Peter ("the Messiah, the Son of the living God") and a resounding praise of Peter by Jesus:

> Blessed are you, Simon Bar-Jonah! For flesh and blood has not revealed this to you but my Father who is in heaven. And I tell you, you are Peter; and on this rock I shall build my Church, and the gates of Hades will not prevail against it. I shall give to you the keys of the kingdom of heaven. Whatever you bind on earth will be bound in heaven; whatever you loose on earth will be loosed in heaven.

How can we explain such a discrepancy? The suggestion once popular among Catholics that Mark (and Luke) had abbreviated the Matthean scene has little following today now that Catholics are no longer bound to follow the Roman Biblical Commission directive that Matthew was the first Gospel, written by an eyewitness.[61] Why would Mark have felt free to omit such an important statement by Jesus, the only passage in the Gospels where the idea of Church occurs?[62] But if Matthew has added

[61]See footnote 54 above.
[62]See footnote 39 above.

material to the Marcan scene, from where did he obtain it? There are noticeable similarities between the Matthean passage and the language that Paul used to describe his post-resurrectional experience of Jesus (Gal 1:16: "reveal," "Son," not "flesh and blood"). And so there is good reason to think that Matthew has added to the traditional confession by Peter at Caesarea Philippi an echo of the appearance of the risen Jesus to Peter (I Cor 15:5), consisting of Peter's confession of Jesus as Son of God and a church-founding response by the risen Jesus.[63] Both these features, exalted christological confessions and church-founding statements, are associated with post-resurrectional appearances in other Gospels.

The extent to which Matthew gives a portrait of Peter that goes beyond the ministry of Jesus is further emphasized by the peculiar scene in Matt 17:24-27 which begins with the inquiry of the tax collectors to Peter as to whether Jesus pays his taxes. Peter answers yes; but when he encounters Jesus, Jesus reminds him that earthly kings collect taxes from others, not from their sons. Yet in order not to give offense, Peter is to go fishing and catch a fish that would have in its mouth a coin exactly right to pay the tax for Jesus and for Peter. Past discussions of the episode have often centered on the likelihood or historicity of such a miracle which, unlike most of the Gospel miracles, serves the convenience of the miracle worker. But if the scene is examined in the light of later church problems as to whether Christians should in conscience pay Jewish or Roman religious taxes, we can then see Peter getting from Jesus an answer to such a problem. Thus, at the time Matthew is writing, through the imagery of Peter, there is developing or has developed something like an authoritative magisterium to answer new problems facing the Church. This corresponds with Matthew's attribution of the

---

[63]That Catholic scholars could embrace such a theory of Matthew's freely joining two traditions (a ministry confession of Jesus as the Messiah, and a post-resurrectional confession and response) will undoubtedly trouble their co-religionists who have not accepted the affirmation of the Pontifical Biblical Commission (1964; see Appendix): "The truth of the story is not at all affected by the fact that the Evangelists relate the words and deeds of the Lord in a different order and express his sayings not literally but differently."

power to bind and loose to Peter and to the disciples (Matt 18:18).

Another key to how Peter's image was growing after his death comes from an unexpected source, chapter 21 of John which most regard as an addendum to the Fourth Gospel and one of the latest pieces of Johannine composition. It is the well-known story of how the risen Jesus appeared to the disciples while they were fishing on the Sea of Tiberias and how the miraculous catch of fish which he directed catalyzed their recognition of him. Curiously, while the scene centers on the catch of fish to the point of numbering the fish and while Simon Peter hauls the net ashore (21:11), the conversation between Jesus and Peter concerns sheep not fish: "Feed my lambs; tend my sheep." In debate about the Papacy these words have been discussed primarily as to how much authority a shepherd has and whether Peter had authority over other disciples as part of the sheep, while the shift of imagery has often been dismissed as the combination of two different scenes. Be that as it may, the shift from fisherman to shepherd may well reflect the history of Peter's image in the Church. In the earlier days when the missionary enterprise was foremost, Peter the fisherman was acknowledged as the chief missionary among the Twelve, so that in Gal 2:7 Paul compares himself to Peter; and Luke 5:10, in the narrative of the call of the disciples, makes Peter the sole addressee of the directive, "Henceforth you will catch men." (The latter is precisely in the context of the miraculous catch of fish which Luke shares with John 21.) But toward the end of the century, while the missionary enterprise continued, pastoral concern moved into the forefront. The communities won over by the mission had to be cared for; and the language of shepherding and sheep replaced the language of fishing as a symbol for this pastoral task (Acts 20:28-29; I Pet 5:1-5). Accordingly, John 21 evokes the tradition that Jesus addressed Peter not only as a fisherman (found also in the Synoptic Gospels) but also as a shepherd whose task it was to feed the sheep. John 21 was clearly written after Peter had died, for his death as a martyr is mentioned in vs. 18-19; but his image remained adaptable to church needs at the end of the century.

A similar trajectory of image can be traced for other

famous apostolic figures after their death. The Pastoral Epistles were probably written after Paul's death, and in them Paul is no longer primarily a missioner. His concern is exactly like that of the author of I Peter, which may also be posthumous and pseudonymous: to have presbyters in the churches who will be good pastors or shepherds of the flock. (This is also the image that Luke gives to Paul in his farewell address to the presbyters of Ephesus in Acts 20:28-30.) The image of James, the brother of the Lord and the hero of Jewish Christianity, underwent development in the apocryphal literature, and eventually it was claimed that the bishopric of Jerusalem was passed from one brother of the Lord to another.[64]

What happened when the trajectory of one of these apostolic heroes crossed the trajectory of another? An early stage in the encounter of rival trajectories may be found in the Fourth Gospel which stresses the importance of an anonymous figure, "the disciple whom Jesus loved," who was the chief witness behind the community's tradition (John 19:35; 21:24). In order graphically to portray this Disciple's closeness to Jesus, the Fourth Evangelist has centered him in the crucial scenes of Jesus' "Hour": the Last Supper (13:23-26), in the legal process against Jesus (18:15-16), at the crucifixion (19:26-27), at the empty tomb (20:2-10), and at the appearance of the risen Jesus (21:7, 20-23). Almost always the Beloved Disciple appears as a foil to Simon Peter, a backhanded attestation to the importance of Peter as the apostolic witness best known to the Church at large. As a feature of ecclesiastical one-upmanship, the Beloved Disciple comes off in these scenes more favorably than Peter; he is quicker to see, to understand, and to believe because he has a primacy in Jesus' love. But in this Johannine instance of rival trajectories it is interesting that Simon Peter, not the Beloved Disciple, is told to feed the sheep. And the Beloved Disciple is not made a martyr in imitation of Peter, even though it is emphasized that the Disciple's prolonged life was just as much predicted as was Peter's death.

We encounter another instance of rival trajectories in II

---

[64]See *Peter in the New Testament* (footnote 48 above), 47, especially note 109.

Peter. This work, certainly not written by Peter, may be the last of the NT works, composed in the second century. The author is confronted with what he regards (in our terminology) as a misdirected trajectory of Paul's image, for he addresses himself to ignorant and unstable readers of the Pauline letters who are twisting and misconstruing Paul's sayings (3:15-16).[65] One may well suspect that for them Paul is *the* apostle whose letters are supremely authoritative. How does the author counteract this abuse of the apostolic authority of Paul? He calls upon the authority of Peter who speaks magisterially as the interpreter of sacred writings against false prophets (1:20ff.). This interpretation of II Peter as an appeal to one apostle's image in order to correct the (false) appeal to another apostle's image may explain the curious fact that the author bases the authority of Peter on the transfiguration rather than on the appearance of the risen Jesus. If the author said that the risen Jesus had appeared to Peter, his opponents could have replied that Paul too saw the risen Jesus. But they could not claim that Paul was an eyewitness of the majesty of Jesus on the holy mountain when the voice of the Majestic Glory spoke (1:16-18). Thus, we see in II Peter how in one section of Christianity (Rome?[66]), the trajectory of Peter's image began to outdistance the trajectory of Paul's image.

In Rome such outdistancing became even more pronounced. If we look back for a moment to a non-canonical epistle, I Clement, written before II Peter, Peter and Paul are side by side as righteous pillars of the Church (5:2-7)—an interesting adjustment in church architecture since Paul, who once spoke disparagingly of the so-called pillars of the church at Jerusalem (James, Peter, and John) has now been transformed into a church pillar by a Roman writer. Even at the end of the second century, and thus after II Peter, Irenaeus (*Adv. Haer.* III 3:1-2) speaks "of the greatest and very old church in Rome . . . founded by the glorious apostles Peter and Paul." But when the bishopric

---

[65]The fact that the author assumes that his opponents have a collection of Paul's letters is a very important indicator for a date in the second century.

[66]II Peter is directed to the same audience as I Peter (II Pet 3:1), and I Peter is usually thought to have been written from Rome (Babylon in I Pet 5:13).

of Rome emerged as the most prestigious in the Empire, it was primarily in continuity with Peter rather than with Paul that the Roman bishop (e.g., Leo I) was seen to stand in his care for other churches—in continuity with the various roles of Peter in the NT as a fisherman-missionary, as a shepherd-pastor, as a martyr, and a confessor of the faith, and as a magisterial guardian against false teaching.

To sum up, I would assert that the NT study of Peter is shifting from the anachronistic question of whether Jesus appointed Peter as the first Pope to the question of the thrust or the trajectory of the images of Peter even after his death. The First Vatican Council stated that Peter was constituted by Christ the Lord as "the visible head of the whole Church militant" who had "a primacy of true and proper jurisdiction" and who by divine law was to have "perpetual successors" in the Bishops of Rome. In intelligent ecumenical dialogue such statements would have to be judged not simply as to whether they are verifiable in the career of the historical Simon but also as to whether they are true to the trajectory of the imageries of Peter in the NT and beyond. Many a scholar who would not find satisfactory historical evidence for the existence of a visible head of the whole Church militant in Peter's lifetime might have less difficulty in seeing the basis for such a description in the images of Peter that flourished in the last part of the first century after Peter's death. Thus, I see the possibility of approaching from a wider angle the whole question of the relation of the Papacy to Peter: To what extent has the trajectory of Peter's images culminated in the Papacy as it exists today?

A THEOLOGY OF THE PAPACY

But even the question I have just asked may be too narrow for ecumenical discussion, for it may commit Protestants and Catholics to discussing the current functioning of the Papacy as the only possible style of succession to Peter. In such a view the Petrine trajectory would be seen as terminated for better or for worse. But the very notion of a Petrine trajectory in the NT where the image of Peter was adapted to meet the needs of a

Church after his death supposes the possibility of the continued adaptibility of this image to meet the needs of the present Church or the Church of the future. Vatican I spoke of the authority of the bishop of Rome in terms of "full and supreme," "ordinary and immediate" jurisdiction over each and every church and over each and every shepherd and faithful member. If the Papacy one day faces a situation wherein Protestants are open to the Bishop of Rome as a spokesman for a united Church, how could such a concept of jurisdiction be adapted to meet their needs?

Here I reflect the aspect from which the Lutheran—Roman Catholic Dialogue approached the Papacy. In the Dialogue we had previously discussed our common ideas about sacramental ministry to the local churches. We agreed that by God's will a special ministry was needed to preach the Gospel and administer the sacraments to local churches. Now we were going one step farther and asking ourselves: Have we anything to say in common about a special ministry to the Church universal? In other words, we approached the Papacy from the viewpoint of the service that it might render to all Christians and not from the viewpoint of the authority that it claimed over Christians—and that switch is certainly faithful to the spirit of a Jesus who came to serve and warned his followers not to exercise authority over one another as the leaders of the Gentiles did (Mark 10:42-45). Vatican I had spoken of the Pope's jurisdiction over other Christians, but we were looking to Vatican II to see if it might enhance the idea of the Pope's service to other Christians. Jurisdiction may have been a very appropriate expression for Petrine authority in the 19th-century-European context where the legitimate rights and claims of religion were being trampled upon by the emerging national states; but we were asking whether Petrine authority might be formulated with a different emphasis in the growing ecumenical era at the end of the 20th century. (Notice that I say "formulated." As a Catholic I am not questioning the existence of a Petrine authority, but the study of the Petrine trajectory shows how that authority has found different expressions and formulations to meet different Church needs.) Our appeal to the directions inaugurated at Vatican II as a possible guide to a modification of the jurisdictional image of the Papacy projected at Vatican I seemed to be justified by the document *Mysterium Ecclesiae* that I mentioned above[67] which recognized that Church doctrine is sometimes phrased in the changeable conceptions of a given epoch and needs a fuller and more perfect expression at a later time. In particular, we were interested in the possibility of an ecumenically acceptable leadership by the Bishop of Rome if eventually the exercise of his leadership incorporated fully and more perfectly three principles that surfaced at Vatican II: legitimate diversity, collegiality, and subsidiarity.

The Principle of Legitimate Diversity. This principle recognizes that the Spirit's guidance may give rise to diverse forms of theology, law, custom, and piety within the Church. Obviously, the Roman Catholic Church has made progress in tolerating diversity since Vatican II—so much progress that those accustomed to uniformity think the Church is falling apart; and at the Fourth Synod of Bishops in October 1974 the appeal for further diversity, emanating particularly from the Third World bishops, seemed dangerous to the Pope himself. Diversity of piety and of liturgy will probably be accepted more easily than diversity of theology and of canon law. Yet, viewing possible future church union, Protestants would want a respect for legitimate differences in the latter area as well. In my next lecture I shall be dealing with mariology, and that is an area in which we shall probably never see a uniform theology between Protestants and Catholics. In my previous lecture I discussed the possible ordination of women and mentioned the obstacle to ordination raised by the international character of Roman Catholicism: there are areas of Catholicism that are quite unready for a woman as an official preacher or celebrant at the eucharist. But, if that is a main factor, may not diversity be a possible solution: the ordination of women only in those areas that are accustomed to have women in public roles (even as the ordination of married men may be eventually deemed necessary in missionary areas but not in other areas)? Diversity has within

---

[67]See the Appendix for the pertinent excerpt.

itself the danger of promoting division and even separation; but precisely with the Papacy as a strong cohesive force (perhaps the single most powerful force holding us Catholics together), the Roman Church should ideally be able to tolerate more diversity than many other Christian Churches. A Papacy that would respect diversities within Catholicism would be a Papacy with much greater appeal to ecumenical union.

The Principle of Collegiality. The greater sharing of power (and duties) has been a feature of the Roman Catholic Church since Vatican II. In many areas the pastor of the parish is introducing laymen and laywomen into the process of pastoral and administrative decisions. Through diocesan senates priests are beginning to exercise an influence on the decisions of bishops. And at the highest level the Synods of Bishops held every three years in Rome may be beginning to exercise influence on the decisions of the Pope. The approach is cautious; it is usually specified that respectively the parish councils, senates of priests, and Synods of Bishops are only advisory. But psychologically they are more than advisory: it is very difficult for the person in authority consistently to oppose the advice. Therefore, the agencies of collegiality have within them the potentialities of changing the mode of exercising authority within the Roman Catholic Church. Let me mention two instances of the reactions of American bishops to Rome in pastoral matters that I see as significant indicators of the way collegiality may modify the exercise of authority. The privilege of handling many marriage dispensations and dissolutions had been entrusted to the local American bishops, exempting them from submitting such cases to Rome for decision. But in the last two years there were definite indications that Rome was about to curtail this privilege. Many of the American bishops did not think that such a curtailment was in the best pastoral interests of the Church; they felt that it would work an unjustifiable hardship of delay upon their people, often keeping them away from the eucharist for a longer period of time until their marriage case was solved. Perhaps at an earlier period in the century the bishops would have accepted the Roman decision in silence or with mild expression of dissent, but this time they sent a special delegation of bishops to the Pope himself to express their pastoral judgment and request reconsideration—a successful delegation. The bishops were also disturbed by the manner in which there was communicated to them a Roman decision to end an experiment permitting children to receive the sacrament of the eucharist before receiving the sacrament of penance. In this second instance the American bishops found a shrewd, almost Solomonic, way of continuing the experiment: they stressed that instruction for the sacrament of penance should be given to the children, but they insisted on the freedom of the parents to decide which sacrament their children were to receive first. And once more the bishops communicated to Rome their pastoral feelings on the whole subject. To some ultra-conservative Catholics this represented rebellion against the Papacy whose role is seen solely as one of command. But to others such actions foreshadow the type of collegial exchange that should grow up between the local churches and the Papacy. Once again such collegial give-and-take can reshape the functioning of the Papacy so that it may serve effectively Protestant churches which, in any union, would expect a common leader to respect their own pastoral practices.

The Principle of Subsidiarity. Due respect must be given to the importance of the local church, not only by way of allowing it collegial interchange with the centralized Papacy, but even more by way of acknowledging its place in the Christian scheme of redemption. It has often been said that most Catholics view the Church from the top down—a pyramid with sides sloping down from the Pope to bishops to priests to laity. The principle of subsidiarity suggests that we view the Church from the bottom up, with centralized authority seen as rendering a useful service but not as constituting the core of the Church. An anecdote is appropriate here. When groups of priests are in Rome, frequently a visit is arranged for them to the offices of the administrative units of the Church (the Congregations of the Roman Curia); this visit is partly for pedagogical purposes and partly for public relations to improve the image of the administration. On one such visit the Roman prelate who administered the particular office was explaining to a group of American priests how things were done there "at the center of the Church" with an appeal that the principles be properly explained and applied "on the outside." He was interrupted by a puzzled priest who stated that, when he was administering the sacraments to the people in his parish and preaching the Gospel to them, he thought he was at the real center of the Church and that the Roman administrative offices, however necessary, were really on the periphery of what the Church was all about. An oversimplification to be sure, but not without its eloquence in phrasing a different concept of the Church. The principle of subsidiarity, when applied to the functioning of the Papacy, could modify the tendency toward centralization so prominent in the last one hundred years and go far to allay Protestant fears about the possible abuse of unified leadership. No Catholic wants the Pope to become merely the chairperson of the board; on the other hand, a constant stress on monarchical imagery will do little to unify the churches.

I have no certainty if or how the Papacy will eventually restructure itself to give adequate expression to these principles of legitimate diversity, collegiality, and subsidiarity. Such restructuring may take a long time and face many obstacles. Jesus warned his followers of the seduction of power (Luke 22:25-26); and once power has been exercised in a certain manner, the suggestion of other models may be regarded as a threat to the very existence of the power. But the prospects of a renewed Papacy were so exciting to the Lutheran theologians involved in the Lutheran—Catholic Dialogue that they joined with their Catholic confreres in asking the Lutheran churches:

> If they are prepared to affirm with us that papal primacy, renewed in the light of the Gospel, need not be a barrier to reconciliation.
> If they are able to acknowledge . . . the possibility and desirability of the papal Ministry, renewed under the Gospel and committed to Christian freedom, in a larger communion which would include the Lutheran churches.

It is not surprising that very conservative Lutherans accused their scholars in the Dialogue of having sold out to Catholics; what is shocking is that conservative Catholics made the same accusation against the Catholic scholars involved: for them, to invoke the principles of diversity, collegiality, and subsidiarity was to sell out the Papacy.

But there were other reactions that recognized the tremendous advance which had been made. Let me conclude this lecture on the future of ecumenism with regard to Peter and the Papacy by telling you of the reaction of a student at Union Theological Seminary when I gave a public lecture on the subject. She analyzed my report of the progress as seeming to imply a certain amount of give-and-take on both sides; and so she asked me whether in the long run the Papacy did not have to take the first step by illustrating more clearly its acceptance of the three principles I had discussed, before Protestants could begin to see the possibilities of the Papacy for them and their churches. In order to respond fully, I suppose I would need time to think out all the pros and cons of who should take the first step, especially since I am not sure that ecumenical goals are achieved by calculation and I suspect that the side which takes the first bold step will be recognizable as the most Christian. What I did answer on the spur of the moment and what I still feel is that in many ways the greatest corrective to over-centralization in Rome will occur the day a Protestant church comes knocking on the Vatican door to say: "We want corporate union." Over and over again church leaders have said that they hope and pray for unity, but it will be fascinating when someone finally calls the cards so that they have to do something about a concrete bid. Then it will no longer be possible to postpone until the distant future the question of how the Papacy would have to function in a united Church where the Pope would owe as much pastoral allegiance to the Protestant components as to those who had always accepted his leadership. Such a daring request for corporate union might be the ultimate challenge to the successor of Peter, testing what it means to feed the sheep of Jesus in the last quarter of the last century of the second millenium. It has been the Papacy's proudest boast that to Peter alone among all the disciples Jesus gave the power of the keys. A Protestant church asking for corporate union would be asking Peter's successor to use those keys to get the door open.

5.
The Meaning of Modern
New Testament Studies for an
Ecumenical Understanding of Mary

Since Vatican II it has been popular in Roman Catholicism to speak of a hierarchy of truths or dogmas. To theologians this means a gradation of doctrines wherein some are recognized as more central to Christianity than others.[68] In such a hierarchy the topics that I have chosen for these Hoover Lectures would be fairly far down the list. Both the ordaining of women and the Papacy are aspects of Church order or ministry, logically sequential to doctrine about God, Christ, the Spirit, the Church, and ministry in general. The Marian dogmas, except when primarily christological (e.g., Mary as the Mother of God), would also be far down the list, reflecting the application of redemptive grace within the Church to its most prominent citizen. Vatican II recognized this by incorporating the treatment of Mary into its treatment of the Church.

But, to be accurate, we should not speak of a hierarchy of truths but of *hierarchies* of truths. The hierarchy just described makes centrality within the Christian mystery the criterion; but another hierarchy would emerge if one makes the self-identity

---

[68]In the Vatican II document on ecumenism (#11), Catholic theologians engaged in ecumenical dialogue are told that "they should remember that in Catholic teaching there exists an order or 'hierarchy' of truths, since they vary in their relationship to the foundation of the Christian faith."

of a Christian group the criterion; another hierarchy if one makes devotional impact or spirituality the criterion, etc. In a hierarchy based on ecclesiastical identity, an acceptance of the Papacy would be at the very top for Roman Catholics (even as the inspiration of Scripture might be at the top for some Protestants). In a hierarchy based on devotional impact, the Marian dogmas might be near the top for Roman Catholics. (This is reflected unpleasantly in the emotional backlash that often greets Catholic theologians who propose to reexamine the mariological dogmas in the light of historical criticism—the most recent example being the reaction to Avery Dulles' suggestion that the anathemas or condemnations against unbelievers be removed from the statements of the Immaculate Conception and the Assumption.) And so, Mary, like the Papacy, constitutes a point of major concern for the ecumenical future. In the recent attempt to compose an ecumenical catechism,[69] the editors contended that it might be possible for Catholics and Protestants to unite except for their continuing dispute on precisely these two points.

But unlike the Papacy, mariology has not yet been the subject of discussion in the formal ecumenical dialogues between the churches. This means that in this lecture I do not have the advantage I had in the previous lecture, namely, of having engaged with Catholic and non-Catholic confreres in maturing and correcting conversation. More than in the other lectures I am working on an exploratory basis; and the ideas that I advance will be tentative and sketchy, open both to correction and completion. Ecumenism requires a spirit of adventure, and so I invite you to come with me into areas which I have only imperfectly scouted. Yet, in order that there be some context of dialogue for my reflections, I wish to use as a starting point and foil for the lecture the observations of the Lutheran theologian Wolfhart Pannenberg in an article entitled, "Mary, Redemption and Unity."[70] Pannenberg began that article with an eloquent

---

[69]*The Common Catechism* (New York: Seabury, 1975), ed. L. Vischer and J. Feiner, esp. p. 666.

[70]*Una Sancta* 24 (1967), 62-68.

paragraph that might well introduce any ecumenical consideration of Mary:

> Mariology has a central place in ecumenical discussions, or at least should have. The reason is that Mary plays such a large role in the life and piety of the Roman Church, a role which many Protestants believe to be a chief obstacle to realizing Christian unity. Together with the questions of the papacy and of the juridical character of dogma, mariology has high priority on our ecumenical agenda. If we expect Roman Catholics to be flexible and open to change regarding their mariological dogmas, we too must make a much more serious effort to understand structures of thought which seem strange to us. Only in this way can Christians begin to envision a new and truly catholic mariology: a mariology which is neither a foreign imposition upon evangelical thought nor an intolerable break in the continuity of Roman Catholic thought.

As the article proceeds, Pannenberg enters into debate with the Dutch Catholic theologian Eduard Schillebeeckx who had written *Mary, Mother of Redemption*. There are many points in the Pannenberg-Schillebeeckx debate that warrant attention, but toward the end of his article Pannenberg makes a major point that can serve to focus this lecture. He affirms that mariology and christology are or should be very different because Mary is consistently a symbolic character while Jesus is a historical character. "The chief difference between christology and mariology," he states, "is methodologically evident in that christology is the explication of the meaning of an historical event, while mariology attempts to personify the characteristics of the new mankind of faith."[71] He contends that Roman Catholics, including Schillebeeckx, have failed to give sufficient attention to this formal difference. Fundamental to Pannenberg's claim is his contention that we know very few historical facts about Mary. I would like in this lecture to test that affirmation in regard to the NT. I would like to conduct a quest of the historical Mary (or more realistically, a mini-quest) to see how biblical criticism affects the passages in which she features pro-

---

[71] *Ibid.*, 67.

minently. If the quest shows that, in fact, we know very little about the historical Mary, I shall then return to the value of Mary as a symbolic figure and what this means for Christianity and ecumenism.

I shall not attempt to treat every Marian passage in the NT,[72] but I shall comment on the two writings that have most influenced mariological thought, Luke and John. The Lucan infancy narrative containing the annunciation to Mary and the Johannine portrait of the mother of Jesus at Cana and at the foot of the cross have been thought to supply important insights into Mary's role in the life of Jesus and in the mystery of salvation. I have already studied the Johannine passages in my commentary on John,[73] and I am currently engaged in writing a long commentary on the Infancy Narratives of Matthew and Luke;[74] and so I do not need to cover every detail here. Yet I confess that the focus supplied by the historical question about Mary has caused me to see features in Luke and John otherwise missed in a general exegetical treatment.

MARY IN THE GOSPEL OF LUKE

It is well known that in the NT there is no mention of Mary by name outside the four Gospels and one passage at the beginning of Acts. If we look at the earliest NT writings, there is one indirect reference to Jesus' mother in the whole of the Pauline Letters, namely, that he "was born of a woman, born under the Law" (Gal 4:4).[75] If we look at the latest NT writings, there is a possible reference to Mary (one much disputed) in the

---

[72] I have reason to believe that an ecumenical team of scholars will produce a book on *Mary in the New Testament*, similar to *Peter in the New Testament* (footnote 48 above).

[73] *The Gospel According to John* (Anchor Bible 29, 29A; New York: Doubleday, 1966, 1970; London: Chapman, 1971).

[74] To be published by Doubleday, hopefully about 1977.

[75] The description in Rom 1:3, "descended from David according to the flesh," can scarcely be considered a reference to Jesus' descent from Mary; for there is no evidence that Paul knew that Jesus had no human father or that he had a tradition whereby Mary (rather than Joseph) was of the house of David.

symbolic woman of Rev 12 who gives birth to the Messiah.
Thus, the NT quest for the historical Mary is based on the data
in the Gospels.

In the common or Synoptic tradition of the first three Gospels there are only two references to Mary. The *first* reference
simply identifies Jesus as her son. In Mark 6:3 the question is
asked by the citizens of Nazareth, "Is not this the carpenter, the
son of Mary, brother of James, Joses, Judas, and Simon?"
Luke 4:22 has simply, "Is not this Joseph's son?" The text in
Matt 13:55 seems to combine a tradition similar to Luke's with
Mark: "Is not this the carpenter's son? Is not his mother called
Mary? And are not his brothers James and Joseph and Simon
and Judas?" In other words we may be seeing in the Synoptics
the reflections of two sources:[76] a source common to Matthew
and Luke (Q) which read "Is not this Joseph's son?" and a
source behind Mark which read "Is not this the carpenter, the
son of Mary?" Possibly the older reference is the reference to
Jesus as son of Joseph, and the Marcan usage "son of Mary"
reflects the fact that Joseph was forgotten since he was already
dead by the time of the ministry.[77] On the other hand, if one
argues for the antiquity of the "son of Mary" usage, as I would
be inclined to do,[78] we may be hearing echoes of a slurring ref-

---

[76]Are those two sources also reflected in John 6:42 ("Is not this Jesus, the son
of Joseph, whose father and mother we know?")? Or does John represent a
more original reading mentioning both the father and mother which has been
split up in the two Synoptic sources? The possible variations in the oral transmission of such a saying reduce scholars to guessing.

[77]Joseph's name is not even mentioned in Mark. M. Miguens, *Marian Studies*
26 (1975), 43-45, argues that Mark himself changed the "Joseph" of his source
to "Mary" because of his conviction that Jesus had no human father. This is an
implausible use of the argument from silence. Mark nowhere expresses that conviction, and it is really a *tour de force* to suppose that his readers would have
seen such a conviction behind the expression "son of Mary." Miguens makes a
similar deduction from Paul's "born of a woman" (Gal 4:4), so that Paul,
Mark, and John who never mention the virginal conception suddenly become eloquent witnesses of that idea. The fact that John twice speaks of Jesus as "son
of Joseph" (1:45; 6:42) is not seen as a difficulty, although Mark's avoidance of
that expression is a proof of his knowledge of the virginal conception!

[78]It is combined with a reference to Jesus as a carpenter which is scarcely a
late invention. Moreover, if the "son of Mary" is not pre-Marcan, how does one

erence to Jesus' origins, a point I shall raise below in reference
to the virginal conception.

Fortunately the *second* common Synoptic reference gives a
little more information. Let me begin with the scene in Mark 3
which has two parts. (It is important to keep the bipartite nature of the Marcan account carefully in mind.)
(A) In Mark 3:19-21 we are told, "Then Jesus went home; and
the crowd came together again so that they could not even eat.
And when 'his own' heard it, they went out to seize him; for
they said, 'He is beside himself.' " There follows a debate between Jesus and the scribes, which in turn is followed by:
(B) The second part of the Marcan scene (3:31-35):

> And his mother and his brothers came; and standing out-
> side, they sent to him and called. The crowd that was sit-
> ting around him said to him, "Your mother and your
> brothers are outside, asking for you." But he replied,
> "Who are my mother and my brothers?" And looking
> about at those who sat around him, he said, "Here are my
> mother and my brothers! Whoever does the will of God is
> my brother and sister and mother."

The two parts of the Marcan scene are separated by only ten
verses. In the first part "his own" go out to seize him; in the
second part his mother and brothers arrive and ask for him.
Does this mean that Mark identifies the ambiguous "his own"
as his mother and brothers? If so, for Mark, Jesus' mother and
brothers could not understand what he was doing and thought
that he was beside himself. It is interesting that Luke and Matthew both omit the first part of the Marcan scene and have no
such awkward suggestion.[79] The only parallel to such a low es-
timation of Jesus' family would be John 7:5 which reports, "His
brothers did not believe in him." But notice that John does not
attribute disbelief to Jesus' mother. Mark's bipartite scene may

---

explain the reference to the mother in John 6:42 (footnote 76 above) since most
scholars do not posit John's dependence on Mark?

[79]The suggestion that Jesus' mother thought he was beside himself would be
awkward after the Lucan and Matthean infancy narratives wherein Mary knew
who Jesus was from his conception.

well represent the joining of two once independent traditions, one concerning "his own" (perhaps his brothers) and another concerning his mother and brothers.

What is of importance to us is what Luke does with the second part of the Marcan scene, the part that refers specifically to Jesus' mother and brothers. In Mark, Jesus asks "Who are my mother and my brothers?" And looking about at those who sat around him, he says, "Here are my mother and my brothers!" Clearly he is replacing his natural family with a family of believers, those who do the will of God.[80] This replacement is all the more explicable because Mark has already indicated that "his own" think Jesus is beside himself. Luke not only omits the first part of the Marcan scene about "his own" but drastically modifies the second part[81] by omitting the question "Who are my mother and my brothers?" and the replacement statement "Here are my mother and my brothers!" The scene in Luke 8:19-21 reads as follows:

> Then his mother and his brothers approached him, but they could not reach him because of the crowd. He was given the message, "Your mother and your brothers are standing outside, wanting to see you." But he replied, "My mother and my brothers are these who hear the word of God and do it."

The Lucan scene can be interpreted positively: not as if the hearers of the word of God replace Jesus' mother and brothers as his real family (so Mark), but as a statement that his mother

---

[80]Such a replacement is consonant with Jesus' thought in Mark 10:29 about leaving "house or brothers or sisters or mother or father or children or lands for my sake and for the Gospel." Also the "Q" passage in Matt 10:37 ("He who loves father and mother more than me is not worthy of me") and Luke 14:26 ("If anyone comes to me and does not hate his father and mother . . . and brothers and sisters . . . , he cannot be my disciple").

[81]That Luke is modifying Mark and not simply dependent on a different "Q" tradition is suggested by the close agreement of Matt 12:48-50 and Mark 3:33-35. Originally Mark's account may have been put together from two different traditions with 3:35 a separate logion (it is the only reference to "sister" in the whole scene). Luke's omission of a reference to Jesus' sister may be dictated by his interest in keeping this scene harmonious with Acts 1:14 which mentions Jesus' mother and brothers after the ascension.

and his brothers are among his disciples. The physical family of Jesus is truly his family because they hear the word of God. Luke preserves Jesus' insistence that hearing the word of God and doing it is what is constitutive of his family, but Luke thinks that Jesus' mother and brothers meet the criterion. That this is the correct interpretation of Luke's intent is confirmed by Acts 1:14 where, among the 120 "brethren" who constituted the believing community after the resurrection-ascension, Luke lists "Mary the mother of Jesus and his brothers"—the last specific mention of Mary in NT history. It would seem that for Luke Mary and the brothers were disciples of Jesus during the ministry and remained so after the resurrection.

The Lucan modification of the second part of the Marcan scene may supply us the key to how Luke portrays Mary in the story of the annunciation. The infancy narratives are the last frontier for Catholic critical scholarship. Many scholars have written good articles on the subject, but there has been no recent major commentary that would spell out for Catholics, especially English-speaking Catholics, the problems of history and theology in those two narratives. The infancy narratives are truly different from the rest of the Gospel account. The memories of what Jesus said and did during his ministry came down to the evangelists through the channel of apostolic preachers, some of whom had themselves been eyewitnesses.[82] But we have not the slightest evidence of the origins or transmission of the material concerning Jesus' birth—certainly no one would claim that the apostles were eyewitnesses of that material. The problem becomes more acute when we compare the two accounts provided by Matthew and Luke and find them quite different, hard to reconcile with each other, and indeed hard to reconcile with some details we know about the ministry. One theory in circulation among Catholics that has virtually no following among Protestant critical exegetes is that Luke obtained from Mary his story of the events surrounding Jesus' conception and

---

[82]The Instruction of the Pontifical Biblical Commission, *The Historical Truth of the Gospels*, which I have mentioned several times, by its very logic deals only with the ministry of Jesus. (See Appendix.) There is no official Catholic position on the historicity of the infancy narratives.

birth.[83] If so, the infancy narrative would be an important source for historical information about Mary.

Elsewhere[84] I have examined the composition of the annunciation scene in detail; here I shall summarize briefly. (I must presuppose the virtually unanimous conclusion of scholars that, although the infancy narrative tells the story of Jesus' birth, it was in fact composed only after the story of Jesus' ministry, death, and resurrection was known.) The pattern of an angelic annunciation of the birth of a famous salvific figure has clear antecedents in the births of Isaac and Samson. The idea of applying such a pattern to the conception of Jesus probably was anterior to both Matthew and Luke with the result that the tradition of each evangelist shaped the pattern in a different way, Matthew emerging with the story of an annunciation to Joseph, Luke with an annunciation to Mary. The angelic message to Mary in Luke 1:32, 33, 35 is a rephrasing of the OT promise of Nathan to the House of David (II Sam 7:8-16) and of early Christian christological formulas comparable to that found in Rom 1:3-4. For example, when the Lucan angel says, "A *Holy Spirit* will come upon you and *power* from the Most High will overshadow you; therefore the child to be born will called *holy—Son of God*," what we are hearing is an application to Jesus' conception of phrases that Christians once applied to his resurrection: "*Designated Son of God* in *power* according to a *Holy Spirit* [Spirit of Holiness] by resurrection from [of] the dead" (Rom 1:4). I have also contended elsewhere[85] that the

---

[83]Sometimes it is proposed that Luke actually met Mary; other times family tradition is suggested. The basis of the theory is that only Mary was present at the annunciation and so only she would have known what happened; but this argument neglects the possibility that the scene is a Lucan artistic creation.

[84]R. E. Brown, "Luke's Method in the Annunciation Narratives of Chapter One," *No Famine in the Land: Studies in Honor of John L. McKenzie*, ed. J. W. Flanagan and Anita Robinson (Missoula: Scholars' Press, 1975).

[85]R. E. Brown, *The Virginal Conception and Bodily Resurrection of Jesus* (New York: Paulist, 1973; London: Chapman), 52-66, combined with material mentioned in the article cited in footnote 84 above. The case against an intimate family tradition being the source of Luke's or Matthew's knowledge of the virginal conception has been argued strongly by the Catholic scholar A. Vögtle, *Bibel und Leben* 11 (1970), 51-67.

virginal conception (which is a pre-Lucan idea) need not have come to Luke from intimate family memories but may have resulted from a combination of theological reflection and historical fact. The historical fact could have been the public knowledge that Jesus was born early after his parents came to live together, a type of knowledge presupposed in Matthew's account and implied in Luke's account. Among opponents this fact would have produced the calumnious explanation that Jesus was illegitimate, while Christians, reflecting on the revelation that Jesus was God's Son completely free from sin, saw another explanation of the early birth that would do justice to that revelation: Jesus was born of a virgin who conceived through the power of God's Holy Spirit.[86] But let me leave those points for your further reading, and let me concentrate here on Mary's reaction to the annunciation which is a key point in mariology.

In Luke 1:38 Mary responds to the news of Jesus' conception with these words: "Behold the handmaid of the Lord; let it be done to me according to your word." Do we have here the precious *ipsissima verba* of Mary? I have proposed that the rest of the scene is a careful Lucan composition from earlier material; similarly Luke seems to draw these words from the one scene in which Mary appears in the common Synoptic tradition of the ministry—in other words, from the Lucan form of the scene in Mark 3:31-35 where Jesus' mother and his brothers come calling for him. You will remember that Luke interprets positively Jesus' words: "My mother and my brothers are these who hear the word of God and do it." In the infancy narrative Luke dramatizes Mary precisely in those terms in which Jesus spoke of her. "Let it be done to me according to your word" is simply transposing to the first person the affirmation that Jesus' mother heard the word of God and did it.

---

[86]The veracity of the Christian explanation cannot be scientifically proved. This is an area where one's acceptance of divine inspiration and of the authority of traditional Church teaching will play a deciding role. In my own book on the virginal conception (preceding footnote) I have said (p. 35): "I think that according to the usual criteria applied in Roman Catholic theology the virginal conception would be classified as a doctrine infallibly taught by the ordinary magisterium."

This suggestion is reinforced if we press beyond the annunciation to the visitation where Elizabeth is described as blessing and praising Mary. It is noteworthy that in the Lucan account of the public ministry there is not just one saying about Jesus' mother (the parallel to Mark 3:31-35 which I have just discussed) but a second saying for which there is no exact parallel in the other Gospels,[87] namely Luke 11:27-28:

> As Jesus said this, a woman in the crowd raised her voice and said to him, "Fortunate is the womb that bore you and the breasts you sucked." But he said, "Fortunate rather are those who hear the word of God and keep it."

This second Lucan saying seems to have provided the background for Elizabeth's reaction to Mary in the visitation (1:42, 45):

> Blessed are you among women
> and blessed is the fruit of your womb. . . .
> Fortunate is she who believed
> that the Lord's word to her would be fulfilled.

Like the woman in the crowd, Elizabeth praises Mary's physical motherhood (her womb); but since Elizabeth is the vehicle of the prophetic Spirit, Luke gives her further insight so that she also praises Mary's real value as one who hears the word of God with persevering belief—the value Jesus praised in 11:28 in response to the woman. Once again Luke seems to have found his material (and this time even the form of the material: a macarism, "Fortunate is . . .") in what he knew from the tradition of the public ministry.

---

[87]The second scene may be a doublet of the first scene since the key saying has the same contrast between family relationship and hearing the word of God. Even more precisely it may be a doublet (stemming from a pre-Lucan source) of Mark 3:35 if that verse were once a saying transmitted independently of its present context (see footnote 81 above). Although 11:27-28 is found only in Luke, curiously it is more negative in thrust than 8:19-21, the Lucan adaptation of Mark 3:31-35.

[88]Let me remark briefly on the other references to Mary in the infancy narrative. It would be hard to find critical scholarly support for the thesis that the *Magnificat* was composed by Mary or spoken by her on the occasion of the visi-

This finishes our consideration of the area in the Lucan infancy narrative that was most likely to supply additional historical information about Mary[88] or knowledge that would go beyond that supplied by the brief Marcan scene in the ministry. Actually, it seems likely that Luke has drawn upon his rewritten form of the Marcan scene (or a parallel that he may have had to it: the story of the woman in the crowd) and applied its characterization of Mary to the annunciation and visitation. Thus he is presenting us with a profound theological construction but relatively little by way of new historical knowledge.[89] He has made the logical conclusion that Mary in her first encounter with God's word about Jesus would have reacted in a way consonant with the way she acted later in life when Jesus himself was proclaiming God's word. He has shown that she reacted to the revelation of her physical motherhood of the Messiah not by evaluating that as of prime importance, but by subjecting herself to God's word and thus becoming a mother in the sense valued by Jesus.

---

tation. It is a hymn, perhaps of Jewish Christian origin, that Luke has placed on her lips to express plausible sentiments of praise. There is little new about Mary in the birth narrative of 2:1-20, other than the necessary item that it was she who brought forth the child. The statement in 2:19 (see 2:51), "Mary kept with concern all these events, interpreting them in her heart," has been wrongly used to argue that we are dealing in the infancy narrative with the personal remembrances of Mary. It is a rather standard reaction to revelation (Dan 7:28; *Testament of Levi* 6:2) and has no necessary implication of historicity. Later in this lecture I shall return to the story of the finding of the child Jesus in the Temple (2:41-51) and its implications for Mary's relation to Jesus. Here I would note only the difference between the Mary of 2:48-49 who does not seem to know of Jesus' exalted status and the Mary who was told about Jesus by an angel, or the Mary who heard from the shepherds their report of an angelic proclamation about Jesus. Not all the material in the Lucan infancy narrative had the same origin or the same theology. It may occur to some that in a footnote like this I am not doing justice to the magnificent symbolism in Luke's account of Mary. I agree, but I remind the reader that this is a quest of the historical Mary and so I am confining myself to looking for new historical information.

[89]This statement applies to the Marian sections of the annunciation and visitation which have been the subject of my study. As I pointed out, I think that the virginal conception has a historical basis, but that it is more of a christological affirmation than a mariological one.

MARY IN THE GOSPEL OF JOHN

The other evangelical source for possible historical knowledge about Mary that goes beyond the Marcan scene is the Fourth Gospel.[90] There the "mother of Jesus" appears in two significant scenes that have no obvious parallel in the Synoptic tradition,[91] namely, the first Cana miracle where Jesus changed water to wine and at the foot of the cross.

Let us begin with the Cana scene, uniquely important for our historical quest since it is the only scene in the NT account of the ministry in which Jesus and Mary converse. One can fill several library shelves with all that has been written on this miracle story; here I shall have to be arbitrarily selective.[92] Among the many problems raised by the Cana scene, let me mention three. *First*, the miracle has an unusual context. It is worked in Jesus' native Galilean highlands, a geographical context in partial conflict with the Synoptic contention that Jesus did not perform mighty works in his own country except to heal a few sick (Mark 6:5). It is worked in a context of family and friend-of-the-family, for which we have no other example in the Gospel tradition. Jesus' mother expects Jesus to do something about the shortage of wine, indeed seems almost to expect a miracle, although the Gospel specifically lists this as the first of Jesus' signs (2:11). Finally, the miracle is worked before Jesus goes to Capernaum (see John 2:12), and the movement to Capernaum marks the beginning of the ministry in the Marcan tradition (Mark 1:14-21). *Second*, the miracle is an unusual miracle. I do not mean strange in the sense that it is a nature miracle affecting things rather than people. Such a scholarly distinction has been artificially imposed on a Bible whose God is the God of

---

[90]I shall refer to the evangelist as John. Along with most critical scholars, I do not consider the evangelist to have been John the son of Zebedee. It is debatable whether or not John was the authority upon whom the evangelist drew.

[91]As I pointed out in footnote 76 above, John 6:42 is a parallel to the Synoptic tradition (Mark 6:3 and par.) that Jesus' townsfolk mentioned his parentage.

[92]I am consciously selective in concentrating upon the Marian aspect of a scene which for John is primarily christological. But I contend that it is not illegitimate to ask whether a scene, which admittedly has another focus, tells us anything historical about Mary.

nature as well as of people. Rather I mean that the changing of water to wine does not have the same OT background that marks Jesus' other miracles, including those classified as nature miracles, e.g., the calming of the storm and the multiplication of the loaves. Moreover, it is a miracle worked for the convenience of his mother's friends, and convenience is not a usual characteristic of Jesus' miracles. The miracle may also be deemed strange in the almost incredible abundance of the wine produced (120 gallons). *Third*, the conversation between Jesus and his mother is an unusual conversation, seeming to defy logical interpretation. Apparently Jesus refuses his mother's implicit request about the wine by his reply: "Woman, what has this concern of yours to do with me? My hour has not yet come."[93] Yet Mary acts as if he has acquiesced by telling the waiters, "Do whatever he tells you." And without expressing misgiving or indication of change of mind, Jesus takes care of his host's need for more wine.

Recently, the Anglican scholar Barnabas Lindars[94] has made a suggestion that goes a long way toward solving at least two of the three problems. He uses a form-critical analysis to separate out parts of the Johannine story that have Synoptic parallels. For instance, the saying, "Everyone serves choice wine first; then, when the guests have been drinking a while, the inferior wine," is thought by Lindars to be an authentic saying of Jesus, similar to "No one puts new wine into old wine skins" (Mark 2:23). He thinks that such a saying may once have been enshrined in a parable but has now been attached to a "folk-legend" involving the changing of water to wine. What is new in Lindars' theory[95] is the suggestion that the pre-Johannine folk-

---

[93]An intelligent case can be made for translating the last part of this as "Has not my hour come?" Yet the different translation does not affect my thesis here because the use of "my hour" still involves a separation from Mary's "concern." A. Vanhoye, *Biblica* 55 (1974), 157-67, has argued for the alternative translation; but he says (p. 163) that Jesus is questioning the relationship that had hitherto existed between him and his mother, and will no longer put that relationship on a family level.

[94]B. Lindars, *The Gospel of John* (London: Oliphants, 1972), 126-27.

[95]He acknowledges that the part of his analysis I have already described comes from C. H. Dodd, *The Historical Tradition in the Fourth Gospel* (Cam-

legend (which I prefer to call a popular story since the word legend is often misunderstood) was of the kind found in the apocryphal gospels of Jesus' boyhood where he works miracles in the context of family life. "It is a story of the early life of Jesus while he was still with his mother and brothers." The apocryphal gospels of the boyhood of Jesus, of which *The Infancy Gospel of Thomas* is a good example,[96] appear in the second century, as do the apocryphal gospels of Jesus' infancy. But such apocryphal gospels reflect tendencies that were present in Christian thought or imagination at an earlier date, and we can be certain that individual stories about Jesus' infancy and boyhood were already in circulation in the first century. Earlier material pertinent to the infancy of Jesus is attested in the Gospels of Matthew and Luke, and so it is not at all impossible that boyhood or "hidden life" material might also make its appearance in canonical Gospels. In the Lucan infancy narrative there is appended (2:41-51) a story of Jesus at age twelve which seems to have a quite different origin from the infancy material (see footnote 88 above). In this story the boy Jesus shows marvelous knowledge, much to the amazement of the teachers—exactly the same kind of story found alongside miracles worked for family and friends in *The Infancy Gospel of Thomas*. Thus, the pre-Lucan story of Jesus in the Temple and the pre-Johannine story of a miracle worked at Cana may represent first-century Christian speculation on the "hidden life" of Jesus.

Lindars' suggestion would explain why the Cana story takes place while Jesus is still in the Galilean highlands of his origins, why he is surrounded by his mother and brothers (the

---

bridge Univ., 1963), 227. Those who find shocking the suggestion that a saying once parabolic has been attached to a "folk-legend" may reflect on the fact that Dodd's book is considered quite conservative.

[96]Translated in E. Hennecke and W. Schneemelcher, *New Testament Apocrypha* (Philadelphia: Westminster, 1959), II, 392-401. (This is to be kept distinct from *The Gospel of Thomas* which is part of the Gnostic collection of Chenoboskion.) Despite the name given to it ("infancy Gospel"), it is about Jesus' boyhood, as the author clearly states in his opening paragraph: "I, Thomas the Israelite, tell and make known to you, my Gentile brethren, all the works of the childhood of our Lord Jesus Christ and his mighty deeds which he did when he was born in the land."

latter are mentioned in 2:12), why the miracle is worked for a friend of the family (the wedding is in a nearby village, and Jesus and his mother have been invited), and why the miracle is dated before Jesus' move to Capernaum—a remembrance that this was originally a pre-ministry miracle. It might also explain the almost magical quality of the miracle and the exuberant amount of wine (to which the evangelist will attach symbolic meaning). In the apocryphal gospel tradition the boy Jesus supplies his father Joseph with 100 measures of wheat from sowing one grain and miraculously supplies his mother with water.

But I would like to push beyond Lindars' suggestion about the origin of the story to the dialogue between Jesus and his mother which his theory does not adequately explain. Using a careful method to distinguish between pre-Johannine elements and Johannine editing, Robert Fortna has attempted to reconstruct the pre-Johannine miracle stories.[97] Here is a translation from the Greek of the first part of his reconstruction of the Cana story (omitting the signs by which he indicates varying degrees of probability):

> Now there was a wedding at Cana of Galilee and the mother of Jesus was there. Jesus himself and his disciples had also been invited to the wedding celebration. But they had no wine, for the wine provided for the wedding banquet had been used up. The mother of Jesus told the waiters, "Do whatever he tells you." There were at hand six stone water jars, each one holding 15 to 25 gallons. "Fill those jars with water," Jesus ordered. . . .

In this pre-Johannine stage as reconstructed by Fortna there is no awkward dialogue wherein Jesus seems to refuse his mother.

---

[97] R. T. Fortna, *The Gospel of Signs* (SNTS Monograph 11; Cambridge Univ., 1970). In an evaluation of Fortna's work for the 1969 meeting of the Society of Biblical Literature, I agreed with many points in his methodology and a number of the conclusions, but I expressed doubt that we could reconstruct a whole pre-Johannine Gospel as Fortna had done. But I have consistently maintained that our best evidence for a pre-Johannine *collection* of material was in relation to the two Cana miracles that John numbers in sequence (2:11; 4:54). And so I am in considerable agreement with his treatment of this first Cana miracle. See my commentary (footnote 73 above), 194-95.

If the story arose in a context of Jesus' working miracles *en famille*, as Lindars has suggested, it would be natural for Jesus' mother to expect him to work a miracle for the convenience of her friends; and so in the pre-Johannine story Jesus would have granted without hesitation his mother's request. But in bringing this story into the Gospel, John has inserted a saying of Jesus that really runs contrary to the pre-Gospel picture.[98] In this saying Jesus does not accede to his mother's intervention and clearly differentiates his sphere of interest from hers.

This Johannine insertion agrees with the picture of Jesus' relation to his mother that we find in the Marcan and Lucan passages we have discussed, wherein no importance is attributed to physical family relationship and even his mother and brothers must be judged in terms of hearing the word of God and doing it. It is possible, then, that a popular story which arose in a context of Jesus' working miracles for his family and friends before he began his ministry[99] has been corrected by a Gospel understanding that Jesus did not react to his earthly family in such a way. He worked miracles only as part of God's will, the will of his *heavenly* Father, or, as John would put it, as part of the hour. Perhaps the same corrective process explains

---

[98]There are features in the words, "Woman, what has this concern of yours to do with me? My hour has not yet come," that suggest that they were composed by the evangelist. Jesus addresses his mother as "Woman" again in 19:26, a passage which is scarcely pre-Johannine since the Beloved Disciple, the Johannine character par excellence, is present. Also the use of the "hour" is characteristic of John.

[99]Roman Catholics who are familiar with the emphasis in Pope Pius XII's encyclical *Divino Afflante Spiritu* (1943; see Chapter One above) should have no difficulty with the suggestion that a popular story could find its way into the Gospel tradition. It is no obstacle to an acceptance of the inspiration of the Scriptures. Since the encyclical stresses the existence of different types of literature in the Bible, there is no reason why, alongside inspired history, one could not have inspired fiction or inspired popular narrative. One must use the best scholarly technique to determine what type of literature one is dealing with; and it is precisely in the material pertinent to Jesus' infancy and youth, for which we have no apostolic eyewitness, that one would be most likely to encounter stories with folk origin. But for such stories to become Scripture, to become a written vehicle of God's message, they had to undergo the chastening of true Gospel insight. The evangelist is not responsible for the origin or historicity of the story; he is responsible for the message it serves to vocalize.

the final form of the Lucan story of the boy Jesus in the Temple. The basic story about the marvelous knowledge of the boy Jesus was modified by a dialogue rejecting family interference. To the mother who implicitly rebuked him ("Son, why have you treated us so? Behold your father and I have been seeking you anxiously"), Jesus responds by pointing out that his true family relationship is to God ("How is it that you sought me? Did you not know that I must be in my Father's house [or about my Father's business]?"). The dialogue at Cana is remarkably similar. First, Mary's implicit request for wine is answered with a question emphasizing Mary's misunderstanding, "Woman, what has this concern of yours to do with me?", matching the Lucan "How is it that you sought me?" Then comes Jesus' affirmation of priorities in relation to God: "My hour has not yet come," matching the Lucan "Did you not know that I must be in my Father's house [or about my Father's business]?"[100]

What does all this mean for our quest of the historical Mary? It means that in the Cana story the dialogue between Jesus and Mary (which may have been introduced by John into a pre-Johannine popular story) is nothing more than another form of the tradition common to the Synoptics. It is worded in another way (a Johannine way), but the import is the same: Jesus is approached by his mother (presumably in the presence of the brothers mentioned in 2:12) with a request. He rejects this, referring to the hour (appointed by God), even as in the Synoptic tradition he talks about hearing the word of God and doing it. The evangelist, of course, develops further symbolism from the scene, symbolism primarily concerning Jesus but also concerning Mary (e.g., her role as the "woman"). But in terms of our quest for historical information about Mary, Cana adds little to the general Gospel picture.

Let us turn to the second Johannine scene involving Mary's presence at the foot of the cross. This scene at the end of the ministry is related to the first of Jesus' signs at Cana. The hour of Jesus has now come (13:1), and the woman now reappears.

---

[100]The resemblance between John and Luke is even closer if one should read John's Greek as a question, "Has not my hour come?" (see footnote 93 above).

Once more she is introduced not by name but by title, "the mother of Jesus." It is striking that John never uses her personal name "Mary." John is not shy of personal names: "Mary" occurs some fifteen times in the Fourth Gospel—for Mary the sister of Martha, for Mary Magdalene, for Mary the wife of Clopas, but never for the mother of Jesus. The fact that at the foot of the cross she appears alongside the other great unnamed figure of the Gospel, "the disciple whom Jesus loved," and is put into direct relationship to him is an important key to the scene.

This man had symbolic value for the Johannine community but was not a pure symbol. He was a companion of Jesus and served the Johannine community as its witness for the Jesus tradition. In the previous lecture on Peter (Chapter Four), I pointed out how often he appears in the Gospel alongside Simon Peter, coming off more favorably than the best known of the Twelve. But here I am interested in the historicity of his appearances. The introduction of the Beloved Disciple in the scenes where he appears is almost a Johannine *tour de force*. At the Last Supper we know of the companions of Jesus from the Synoptic tradition, and Peter and Judas play the feature roles in the dialogue about betrayal; but in the Fourth Gospel the Beloved Disciple appears alongside them, close to Jesus (13:23-26). The Synoptic Gospels tell with some detail how Peter followed Jesus after the arrest but denied him in the courtyard or palace of the high priest; only in John (18:15-16) is there present "another disciple" who introduces Peter into the palace. Luke 24:12 tells us how, on the information of the women, Peter ran to the tomb, looked in, and saw the linen cloths; only in the Fourth Gospel does the Beloved Disciple appear as Peter's companion in the visit to the tomb. The appearance of the Beloved Disciple is almost an *intra*-Johannine problem in ch. 21. The author (21:2) has given a list of those who go fishing: Simon Peter, Thomas the Twin, Nathanael, the sons of Zebedee, and two others. From that list one would never suspect that the Beloved Disciple was along; yet after the miraculous catch of fish he is suddenly present, once more alongside Peter. Granted that the Beloved Disciple was a historical figure, are we dealing with history when he keeps turning up in important scenes where other tradition provides no place for him? One of the world's most prominent Johannine scholars, the German Catholic Rudolf Schnackenburg,[101] has suggested that, while the Beloved Disciple was a companion of Jesus, he was not one of the Twelve. But his pupils and friends felt strongly that he should be included in the inner circle of Jesus' disciples and dramatized this feeling by placing him prominently in scenes associated with the Twelve, especially with Peter. Schnackenburg says that, considered from the historical point of view, the Beloved Disciple was "certainly not present" at the Last Supper, even though on a higher theological level the scene expresses the truth of Jesus' relation to him. I would not be so certain, but this serious historical problem had to be mentioned before I could turn to his presence at the foot of the cross.

The other Gospels never mention any male disciple of Jesus at the crucifixion; rather they are specific that the male disciples had forsaken him and fled (Mark 14:53)—a tradition that is echoed in the Fourth Gospel itself: "The hour is coming, indeed it has come, when you will all be scattered, every man to his home, and will leave me alone" (16:32). The only exception to this tradition is the surprising appearance of the Beloved Disciple at the crucifixion in John 19:26, "Jesus saw his mother and the disciple whom he loved standing near"—a scene followed by the Disciple's witness to the water and blood flowing from the side of the dead Jesus in 19:35. Historically, was the Beloved Disciple present? The situation is complicated by the presence of the other titled figure, "the mother of Jesus"; for the Synoptic Gospels are specific that the women stood at a distance (Mark 15:40) and thus not at the foot of the cross. Moreover, Mark and Matthew mention the women by name (Mary Magdalene, Mary the mother of James and Joses, and Salome) without ever mentioning the mother of Jesus. And so in John we are faced with the appearance at the cross of two figures, both never referred to by name, both of symbolic value, for whose presence the Synoptic tradition leaves little room.

Be that as it may, what interests me here is the saying of

---

[101]R. Schnackenburg, "On the Origin of the Fourth Gospel," *Perspective* 11 (1970), 239-40.

Jesus with regard to his mother: he makes her the mother of the Beloved Disciple. The woman whose request he rejected at Cana is now brought into *family* relationship with the ideal disciple. Let me sum up the picture we saw in the other Gospels so that what I am suggesting for John may be clear. In Mark, Jesus rejected any family claim on him stemming from blood ties; he substituted for the physical family a family based on discipleship (doing the will of God). Luke also reports this contrast between physical-family claims and a family constituted by discipleship; but Luke sees the physical family becoming disciples: Jesus' mother and brothers are true family because they hear the word of God and do it. He dramatizes this by bringing Jesus' mother and brothers back on the scene as disciples after the ascension (Acts 1:14). I think John has gone the same route with reference to the mother of Jesus. (And the reason why he insistently calls her "the mother of Jesus" may be precisely because he is interpreting a tradition about what constituted her true motherhood.) At Cana John reported his version of Jesus' rejection of physical-family or maternal claims; but now at the foot of the cross he shows that Jesus does give Mary a role, not as his physical mother but as the mother of the Beloved Disciple. Similarly Jesus stresses that the Beloved Disciple is her son, and thus logically his own true brother. The Johannine Jesus has reinterpreted who his mother and his brother are and reinterpreted them in terms of discipleship.[102] If Luke brought back the mother and brothers of Jesus as disciples after the ascension, John chooses the moment when Jesus has been lifted up (12:32) to bring onto the scene the mother of Jesus who is made the mother of the Beloved Disciple (now Jesus' brother).

*   *   *

And so you see where I have come at the end of this tenta-

---

[102]Those familiar with the Fourth Gospel may object that discipleship is not the only or perhaps even the primary symbolism for the role of Mary at the foot of the cross. I agree, and in my commentary I have made other suggestions. Here, however, I am interested only in the relationship of the Johannine scene to the Synoptic tradition about Jesus' mother and brothers in order to determine whether new historical information is present.

tive discussion of the Lucan infancy narrative and the Fourth Gospel, the two possible major sources for historical information about Mary that would go beyond the one Marcan scene concerning his true mother and brothers. I find that both Luke and John have reworked the Marcan information (or information similar to Mark's) in a way that confirms that Mary is truly a mother, not merely because of physical relation to Jesus, but because she is a true disciple faithful to the word of God. Luke accomplished this by rewriting the Marcan scene itself and by anticipating the portrait of Mary in the annunciation and visitation. From her first encounter with God's will whereby she was to have the role of a mother in the plan of salvation, Mary declared her discipleship in terms of obedience to God's word. John accomplished this partially at Cana, his equivalent to Mark's account of Jesus' rejection of family interference, and partially at the foot of the cross where Mary receives from Jesus her role as mother in God's plan of salvation, mother of the Beloved Disciple who becomes Jesus' true brother. If these observations are correct, I find confirmed more than I had ever expected Pannenberg's contention that the NT does not give us much knowledge of Mary as a historical character.[103]

What are we to say, then, of his contention that symbol-

---

[103]Some Roman Catholics may have expected me to include a discussion of the historicity of the Immaculate Conception and of the Assumption of Mary. But these Marian doctrines, which are not mentioned in Scripture, clearly lie outside my topic which was the quest for historical knowledge of Mary in the NT. Moreover, I would stress the ambiguity of the term "historicity" when applied to these two doctrines. A Roman Catholic must accept the two dogmas as true upon the authority of the teaching Church, but he does not have to hold that the dogmas are derived from a chain of historical information. There is no evidence that Mary (or anyone else in NT times) knew that she was conceived free of original sin, especially since the concept of original sin did not fully exist in the first century. The dogma is not based upon information passed down by Mary or by the apostles; it is based on the Church's insight that the sinlessness of Jesus should have affected his origins, and hence his mother, as well. Nor does a Catholic have to think that the people gathered for her funeral saw Mary assumed into heaven—there is no reliable historical tradition to that effect, and the dogma does not even specify that Mary died. Once again the doctrine stems from the Church's insight about the application of the fruits of redemption to the leading Christian disciple: Mary has gone before us, anticipating our common fate.

ism, not history, is the key to mariology. To some that may seem an impoverishment, but Pannenberg himself insists that there is nothing impoverished about symbolism. It has as much value as history but a different kind of value.

There is in the Christian ethos a deep need that the revelation incarnate in the ministry of Jesus be somehow made personal today. If the genius of God's plan of incarnation was that men and women might see God's will lived out in a life that was just like their own in everything except sin, the very force of that pedagogy creates a necessity to keep the incarnate revelation relevant to the changing conditions of human history. We want not simply to look back and to say that is the way it was but somehow to be able to say that is the way it is or should be today. We see this urge to update the human expression of God's will in the constant attempts to modernize Jesus and make him fit into our culture and life patterns. Yet because we have substantial knowledge of the historical Jesus, of what he did and said, he is modernized with peril.[104] One can and must "follow" Jesus by translating into present-day terms the challenge of his proclamation and example; but it is difficult to contemporize Jesus himself, making him a symbol. He is obviously ill dressed when he appears in the garb supplied by modern imagination, whether that garb be flowing white robes with a halo or the jazzy colors of the hippie rock singer.

But precisely because we do not know much about the historical character and individuality of Mary, she lends herself more freely than Jesus does to a symbolic trajectory. She has been adaptable in various times and places, establishing a relationship between the ministry of Jesus and what it means to be a Christian later and elsewhere. If my interpretation is correct, the evangelistś Luke and John took the first step in this direction by bringing into the conception and the crucifixion of Jesus

---

[104]In genuine Christian theology the great updater of Jesus is the Holy Spirit. The Second Person of the Trinity became incarnate in a particular time and particular place; the Third Person did not. As the Spirit of Jesus, he can make Jesus present to all times and places. Nevertheless, the Spirit, invisible in himself, is visible only in and through the Christian believer; and so we need models of how Jesus can be made visible in disciples at other times and other places. This need explains the Church's presentation of saints for emulation.

(and thus the beginning and end of Jesus' life) the fundamental Marian symbolism—she appears as a disciple both at the annunciation and at the foot of the cross. In later ages the Church constantly turned to Mary to meet the ever-changing aspects of Christian discipleship, translated into terms of virtue and piety. In the Constantinian period, when the threat of martyrdom had passed and the ideal of carrying one's cross was beginning to find expression in asceticism, Mary became the model of women who were withdrawing into the Egyptian desert to lead a cenobitic life. Both Athanasius and a Coptic document that appears in the proverbs of the Council of Nicaea[105] describe Mary as a perfect Egyptian nun who ate and slept only when her body demanded it, modulated her voice, shut her eyes when dressing and undressing, avoided her relatives and even other women who spoke of the things of this world, and who made progress every day. In the Middle Ages Mary became the fair lady of the knights, "our Lady," the symbol of chaste love. In the Renaissance she became the tender mother caring for her spiritual children. In this century she was exalted as part of the Holy Family, that model family of Nazareth which was the Church's rebuttal to divorce and lax morals. And most recently she has been hailed by the American Bishops as the model of the liberated woman.[106] One cannot historicize all these diverse and even contrary pictures of Mary; but in having her assume these symbolic roles, the Church has been contemporizing the ideal of Christian discipleship. The Church has been diagnosing a way in which Christians of various times needed to hear the word of God and keep it. As Pannenberg says,[107] "It is quite understandable why the Church saw itself and its faith-relationship to God and to Christ expressed in Mary rather than in some other figure."

When I began this lecture, I said that mariology was high

---

[105]Hilda Graef, *Mary, A History of Doctrine and Devotion* (London: Sheed and Ward, 1963), 50ff.

[106]*Behold Your Mother,* a pastoral letter from the National Conference of Catholic Bishops of the U.S.A., issued on Nov. 21, 1973, #142: "The dignity which Christ's redemption won for all women was fulfilled uniquely in Mary as the model of all feminine freedom."

[107]The article cited in footnote 70 above, p. 67.

in the emotional hierarchy of dogmas, and that scientific discussion of mariology, no matter how responsible, is likely to arouse vehement reaction among some Roman Catholics. I can well imagine that this lecture in which I have discussed mariology in an ecumenical context may embitter some of my coreligionists, especially since I have agreed with a Protestant theologian that symbolism (specifically a symbolism of discipleship) may be a more fruitful approach to Mary than history. And so I would like to quote a Catholic authority who in his own way has said the same thing as Pannenberg and has eloquently affirmed all that I have said here about discipleship as the fundamental Gospel picture of Mary:

> The Virgin Mary has always been proposed to the faithful by the Church as an example to be imitated not precisely in the type of life she led, and much less for the socio-cultural background in which she lived and which today scarcely exists anywhere. Rather, she is held up as an example to the faithful for the way in which in her own particular life she fully and responsibly accepted the will of God, because she heard the word of God and acted on it, and because charity and a spirit of service were the driving force of her actions. She is worthy of imitation because she was the first and the most perfect of Christ's disciples.

The words quoted are those of Pope Paul VI.[108]

I wish to close these Hoover Lectures on the future of ecumenism by stressing the positive possibilities for all Christians in the understanding of Mary's role that I have sketched. The future of ecumenism is not fully predictable because it is not a question of human mergers or bargaining but a sign of God's action among His people. I believe that the desire for union is the reflection of God's speaking to us in our time. As we face this uncertain future, so dependent on our not placing obstacles to the divine challenge to be one, we can have no better symbol than that of Mary whose whole career is summed up in the simple acceptance of God's will: "Let it be done to me according to your word."

---

[108]*Marialis Cultus*, an Apostolic Exhortation on Devotion to the Blessed Virgin (February 1974), #35.

Appendix:
Some Roman Biblical and Theological Statements Which Have Opened the Church to Change

In Chapter One I mentioned the Roman Catholic Church's opposition to biblical criticism in the first part of the twentieth century, largely through the decrees of the Pontifical Biblical Commission (1905-15). That opposition, although long past, has left an impression, both within and without, that the Church always speaks conservatively and that progress is made only by moving subtly against authoritative positions. But again and again in this book I have based my contentions and my hopes on the progressive directions that have come from authoritative Roman Catholic sources. Instead of scattering the text of these sources, I thought it might be helpful to gather them in an appendix so that the reader could see their impact. For a church that was one of the slowest to accept biblical criticism, the Roman Catholic Church has now some of the most liberal official statements on the subject.

I do not wish to hide the fact that progress in biblical matters has not been linear or without occasional retrogressions. The encyclical of Pope Leo XIII *Providentissimus Deus* (1893) had a more open attitude than the encyclical *Spiritus Paraclitus* (1920) of Pope Benedict XV. The Pius XII who gave biblical criticism its Catholic magna carta in *Divino Afflante Spiritu* (1943) also issued *Humani Generis* (1950), an encyclical largely condemnatory of modern theological movements. Just prior to the liberalizing instruction on Gospel historicity (1964) which I shall quote below, there was a negative warning from the Holy Office on the subject (1962). Catholics whose concept of theology centers around the repetition and defense of church statements can find as many negative statements as I have found positive ones. But the swapping and counterposing of statements from the magisterium is just about as fruitful as inter-Christian apologetics conducted on the basis of exchanging "proofs" from Scripture. Exegesis and intelligent evaluation are as important in reading church documents as in reading the Bible, and there are fundamentalists in both fields. Even if *Humani Generis* of Pius XII was issued with the same authority as the great encyclicals of Pius XII on the Bible, the Church, and the liturgy, it was the Pope of the latter documents whose spirit moved Vatican II. It was the liberal Biblical Commission document on Gospel historicity, not the conservative Holy Office warning, that set the tone for the final decree of Vatican II. Many of the church documents of this century are archival memories; the ones I quote below are "alive and well" in their actual influence on biblical study and theology.

With a minor exception I shall not include quotations from the best known liberalizing documents, *Divino Afflante Spiritu* and the decrees of Vatican II, for these are easily available.[109] I wish to make available the crucial sections of lesser known and less available documents.

* * *

A Declaration of Freedom with regard to the Early Decrees of the Pontifical Biblical Commission (1955). The Roman Catholic Church rarely calls attention to its changes of mind by stating openly that previous positions have been abandoned or previous statements are "inoperative." It lets them die out from memory. And so it was a major concession when the Secretary and Sub-secretary of the Pontifical Biblical Commission clarified

---

[109]See *Rome and the Study of Scripture* (rev. ed.; St. Meinrad, Ind.: Grail, 1962); *The Documents of Vatican II*, ed. W. M. Abbott and J. Gallagher (New York: Guild, 1966).

the status of the conservative decrees issued by the Commission in the period 1905-15 to which, up to that time, Catholic scholars were "bound in conscience to submit." They did this by commenting on the republication of a collection of church statements about Scripture *(Enchiridion Biblicum)*. I have italicized the crucial lines in this excerpt:[110]

> Inasmuch as it is a collection of documents which show how Sacred Scripture has always been the primary source and foundation of the truths of Catholic faith and of their progress and development, the *Enchiridion* renders great service first of all to the history of dogmas. It reflects clearly, moreover, the fierce battle that the Church at all times has had to fight, though with varying degrees of intensity, to maintain the purity and truth of the Word of God. Especially in this respect the decrees of the Pontifical Biblical Commission have great significance. However, *as long as these decrees propose views which are neither immediately nor mediately connected with truths of faith and morals, it goes without saying that the scholar may pursue his research with complete freedom* and may utilize the results of his research, provided always that he defers to the supreme teaching authority of the Church.
>
> Today we can hardly picture to ourselves the position of Catholic scholars at the turn of the century, or the dangers that threatened Catholic teaching on Scripture and its inspiration on the part of liberal and rationalistic criticism, which like a torrent tried to sweep away the sacred barriers of tradition. At present the battle is considerably less fierce; not a few controversies have been peacefully settled and many problems emerge in an entirely new light, so that it is easy enough for us to smile at the narrowness and constraint which prevailed fifty years ago.

The Historical Truth of the Gospels, an Instruction of the Pontifical Biblical Commission (1964). The occasion for this document was the defeat of a very conservative Schema on Divine

---

[110]An English translation (along with the Latin and German originals) and commentary are found in the *Catholic Biblical Quarterly* 18 (1956), 23-29. A translation may also be found in *Rome and the Study of Scripture* (preceding footnote), 175-76, but the reader should be cautioned that the 1962 edition has badly mistranslated the crucial sentence, omitting the key words "complete freedom"!

Revelation submitted to the Second Vatican Council in 1962. That schema had been drawn up by forces in Rome hoping to repeal the biblical reforms of Pius XII and thus restore the situation to 1910. (The anti-Modernist documents of the 1910 period were freely quoted in the schema.) After the defeat of the schema a new drafting committee was commissioned. Their work was considerably facilitated by the issuance of this Instruction by the Biblical Commission with the approval of Pope Paul VI. I quote here only the section pertaining to the formation of the Gospels,[111] with the addition of division headings and italicization. By way of brief commentary, Stage One recognizes a limited worldview on Jesus' part, even if it delicately attributes this to accommodation. Most Catholic scholars would speak more openly of Jesus' own limited knowledge rather than of his accommodating himself to the limited knowledge of his time. Stage Two recognizes that the christology of the early Church was post-resurrectional in origin and was read back into the accounts of the ministry. It allows for development within the pre-Gospel stage of the Jesus tradition, and is a stage of formation close to what scholars isolate by form-critical analysis. Stage Three acknowledges considerable freedom of authorship by the evangelists. It is a stage of formation close to what scholars isolate by redaction criticism. Note that the Roman Catholic Church has gone on record stating that the Gospels are not literal or chronological accounts of the words and deeds of Jesus.

VI. 2. To judge properly concerning the reliability of what is transmitted in the Gospels, the interpreter should pay diligent attention to the three stages of tradition by which the doctrine and the life of Jesus have come down to us.

Stage One: The Ministry of Jesus

VII. Christ our Lord joined to himself chosen disciples, who followed him from the beginning, saw his deeds, heard his words, and in this way were equipped to be witnesses of his life and doctrine. When the Lord was orally explaining

---

[111]For the translation of the whole and a commentary see J. A. Fitzmyer, *Theological Studies* 25 (1964), 386-408.

his doctrine, *he followed the modes of reasoning and of exposition which were in vogue at the time.* He accommodated himself to the mentality of his listeners* and saw to it that what he taught was firmly impressed on the mind and easily remembered by the disciples. These men understood the miracles and other events of the life of Jesus correctly, as deeds performed or designed that men might believe in Christ through them, and embrace with faith the doctrine of salvation.

Stage Two: The Preaching of the Apostles

VIII. The apostles proclaimed above all the death and resurrection of the Lord, as they bore witness to Jesus. They faithfully explained his life and words, while taking into account in their method of preaching the circumstances in which their listeners found themselves. *After Jesus rose from the dead and his divinity was clearly perceived*, faith, far from destroying the memory of what had transpired, rather confirmed it, because their faith rested on the things which Jesus did and taught. Nor was he changed into a "mythical" person and his teaching deformed in consequence of the worship which the disciples from that time on paid Jesus as the Lord and the Son of God. On the other hand, there is no reason to deny that *the apostles passed on to their listeners what was really said and done by the Lord with that fuller understanding which they enjoyed*, having been instructed by the glorious events of the Christ and taught by the light of the Spirit of Truth. So, just as Jesus himself after his resurrection "interpreted to them" the words of the Old Testament as well as his own, *they too interpreted his words and deeds according to the needs of their listeners*. "Devoting themselves to the ministry of the word," they preached and made use of various modes of speaking which were suited to their own purpose and the mentality of their listeners. For they were debtors "to Greeks and barbarians, to the wise and the foolish." But these modes of speaking with which the preachers proclaimed Christ must be distinguished and (properly) assessed: catecheses, stories, testimonia, hymns, doxologies, prayers—and other *literary forms* of this sort which were in Sacred Scripture and were accustomed to be used by men of that time.

Stage Three: The Writing by the Evangelists

IX. This primitive instruction, which was at first passed on by word of mouth and then in writing—for it soon happened that many tried "to compile a narrative of the things" which concerned the Lord Jesus—was committed to writing by the sacred authors in four Gospels for the benefit of the churches, with a method suited to the peculiar purpose which each (author) set for himself. *From the many things handed down they selected some things, reduced others to a synthesis, (still) others they explicated as they kept in mind the situation of the churches.* With every (possible) means they sought that their readers might become aware of the reliability of those words by which they had been instructed. Indeed, from what they had received the sacred writers above all selected the things which were suited to the various situations of the faithful and to the purpose which they had in mind, and adapted their narration of them to the same situations and purpose. Since the meaning of a statement also depends on the sequence, the Evangelists, in passing on the words and deeds of our Saviour, explained these now in one context, now in another, depending on (their) usefulness to the readers. Consequently, let the exegete seek out the meaning intended by the Evangelist in narrating a saying or a deed in a certain way or in placing it in a certain context. *For the truth of the story is not at all affected by the fact that the Evangelists relate the words and deeds of the Lord in a different order, and express his sayings not literally but differently,* while preserving (their) sense. For, as St. Augustine says, "It is quite probable that each Evangelist believed it to have been his duty to recount what he had to in that order in which it pleased God to suggest it to his memory—in those things at least in which the order, whether it be this or that, detracts in nothing from the truth and authority of the Gospel. But why the Holy Spirit, who apportions individually to each one as He wills, and who therefore undoubtedly also governed and ruled the minds of the holy (writers) in recalling what they were to write because of the pre-eminent authority which the books were to enjoy, permitted one to compile his narrative in this way, and another in that, anyone with pious diligence may seek the reason and with divine aid will be able to find it."

X. Unless the exegete pays attention to all these things which pertain to the origin and composition of the Gospels and makes proper use of all the laudable achievements of recent research, he will not fulfil his task of probing into what the sacred writers intended and what they really said. From the results of the new investigations it is apparent that *the doctrine and the life of Jesus were not simply reported for the sole purpose of being remembered, but were "preached" so as to offer the Church a basis of faith and of morals.* The interpreter (then), by tirelessly scrutinizing the testimony of the Evangelists, will be able to illustrate more profoundly the perennial theological value of the Gospels and bring out clearly how necessary and important the Church's interpretation is.

The Statement of Vatican II on Inerrancy (1965). The final decree of Vatican II on Divine Revelation (the Constitution *Dei Verbum*) drew heavily on the preceding document for its treatment of the Gospels. In many other biblical matters it repeated the *status quo* achieved under Pius XII, and in regard to the inspiration of the Scriptures it simply reiterated past positions. But one can detect a significant movement with regard to inerrancy. Inerrancy is a correlary of inspiration: it has been repugnant to Christians to posit error in a Bible for which God had an author's role and responsibility. Only gradually have we learned to distinguish that while all Scripture is inspired, all Scripture is not inerrant. The first step in narrowing the scope of inerrancy is to recognize that the concept is applicable only when an affirmation of truth is involved. In the Bible there are passages of poetry, song, fiction, and fable where the matter of inerrancy does not even arise. A second step is to recognize that not every affirmation of truth is so germane to God's purpose in inspiring the Scriptures that He has committed Himself to it. Already in *Providentissimus Deus* (1893)[112] Pope Leo XIII acknowledged that the scientific affirmations of the Bible were not necessarily inerrant, since it was not God's purpose to teach men science. Eventually the same principle was applied to historical affirmations, but the last frontier has been religious affirmations. Job's denial of an afterlife (Job 14:14-22) makes it difficult to claim that all the religious affirmations of the Bible are inerrant. Vatican II has made it possible to restrict inerrancy to the essential religious affirmations of a biblical book made for the sake of our salvation.[113]

---

[112]For an analysis of this and other Roman documents on Scripture see the article "Church Pronouncements" in *The Jerome Biblical Commentary* (footnote 32 above).

[113]*Dei Verbum* III, 11; *The Documents of Vatican II* (footnote 109 above), 119.

The Books of Scripture must be acknowledged as teaching firmly, faithfully, and without error that truth which God wanted put into the Sacred Writings for the sake of our salvation.

Mysterium Ecclesiae on the Historical Conditioning of Dogma (1973). The battle of biblical criticism has been to get Christians and the Church to recognize that the books of the Bible contain the word of God *phrased in the words of men* and that therefore to discover God's revelation one must take into account the historical situation, the philosophical worldview, and the theological limitations of the men who wrote them. The same battle has to be won in relation to the dogmas of the Church where once again God's revelation has been phrased by men (see Chapter One above). Some found the glimmering of an official acknowledgment of the historical conditioning of dogma in the speech with which Pope John XXIII opened the Vatican Council (Oct. 11, 1962):[114] "The substance of the ancient doctrine of the deposit of faith is one thing, and the way it is presented is another." But a clear affirmation has come a decade later in a document where one might least expect to find it—a declaration of the Doctrinal Congregation (Holy Office) refuting Hans Küng's challenge to infallibility. The document is conservative and the last paragraph in the excerpt I quote below shows that the Church is taking only a hesitant step; nevertheless, the principle of the historical conditioning of dogma has now been accepted. In this excerpt I have added italics and numbered paragraph divisions.[115]

The transmission of divine revelation by the Church encounters difficulties of various kinds. These arise from the fact that the hidden mysteries of God "by their nature so far transcend the human intellect that even if they are revealed to us and accepted by faith, they remain concealed by the veil of faith itself and are, as it were, wrapped in darkness" (Vatican I). *Difficulties also arise from the historical condition that affects the expression of revelation.*

(1) With regard to this historical condition, it must first be observed that *the meaning of the pronouncements of*

---

[114]*The Documents of Vatican II*, 715.
[115]The translation is that of the NC News Service Documentary.

faith depends partly on the expressive power of the language used at a certain point in time and in particular circumstances.

(2) Moreover, it sometimes happens that some dogmatic truth is *first expressed incompletely* (but not falsely), and at a later date, when considered in a broader context of faith or human knowledge, it receives a fuller and more perfect expression.

(3) In addition, when the Church makes new pronouncements, she intends to confirm or clarify what is in some way contained in Sacred Scripture or in previous expressions of Tradition. But at the same time she usually has the intention of *solving certain questions* or removing certain errors. All these things have to taken into account in order that these pronouncements may be properly interpreted.

(4) Finally, even though the truths which the Church intends to teach through her dogmatic formulas are distinct from *the changeable conceptions of a given epoch* and can be expressed without them, nevertheless, it can sometimes happen that these truths may be enunciated by the Sacred Magisterium *in terms that bear the traces of such conceptions*.

In view of the above, it must be stated that the dogmatic formulas of the Church's Magisterium were from the very beginning suitable for communicating revealed truth, and that as they are, they remain forever suitable for communicating this truth to those who interpret them correctly. *It does not follow, however, that every one of these formulas has always been [suitable for communicating truth] or will always be so to the same extent.* For this reason theologians seek to define exactly the intention of teaching proper to the various formulas, and in carrying out this work they are of considerable assistance to the living Magisterium of the Church, to which they remain subordinated. For this reason also it often happens that ancient dogmatic formulas and others closely connected with them remain living and fruitful in the habitual usage of the Church, but with suitable expository and explanatory additions that maintain and clarify their original meaning. In addition, it has sometimes happened that in this habitual usage of the Church *certain of these formulas gave way to new expressions which*, proposed and approved by the Sacred Magisterium, *presented more clearly or more completely the same meaning*.

As for the *meaning* of dogmatic formulas, this remains ever true and constant in the Church, even when it is expressed with greater clarity or more developed. The faithful therefore must shun the opinion, first, that dogmatic formulas (or some category of them) cannot signify truth in a determinate way, but can offer only changeable approximations to it, which to a certain extent distort or alter it; secondly, that these formulas signify the truth only in an indeterminate way, this truth being like a goal that is constantly being sought by means of such approximations. Those who hold such an opinion do not avoid dogmatic relativism, and they corrupt the concept of the Church's infallibility relative to the truth to be taught or held in a determinate way.